The Failure
of Educational Reform
in Canada

The Failure
of Educational Reform
in Canada

edited by Douglas Myers

McCLELLAND AND STEWART LIMITED

Copyright © 1973 McClelland and Stewart Limited

All material in this book is copyrighted and may not be reproduced in any form without permission in writing from the copyright holders.

0-7710-6644-9

McClelland and Stewart Limited
The Canadian Publishers
25 Hollinger Road, Toronto

PRINTED AND BOUND IN CANADA

Contents

Preface

In spite of the title of this informative and provocative collection of articles, educational reform has not failed. What has been called educational reform may have failed, people who have called themselves educational reformers may have failed, but educational reform has not yet been tried. This is not surprising, since it is scarcely understood.

It is easy enough to distinguish between innovation and renovation, although it is only the former that has achieved any significance in educational argot. Innovation is new, novel, with the distinct connotation that it comes from nowhere; it is, as the saying goes, creative, *ex nihilo* almost. It has, therefore, no roots, no connection with the past, and no continuity with the present. In fact, it has only a fleeting future. To label educational activities as innovative is to prepare the way for consigning them to oblivion, and although this is only adumbrated in the meaning of the word, the reality has almost invariably followed. Innovation is a terminal disease, and although it has provided temporary relief for frustrated educators and students, and has acted as a safety valve for the educational system, and although some of the programs have been highly imaginative, it remains true that by its very nature and definition innovation has a brief, giddy, and isolated existence, outside the mainstream of educational activity.

Renovation, a much more promising word, seems to be restricted in its use to physical facilities, the mausoleums of learning. And even in connection with the plumbing and the wiring, the word seems to mean only that what was there originally needs to be replaced. It is a newness of the appearance, and not a newness in the reality; the same old walls are still there, with the same old plaster, and the same old paint, only they have been done over. Renovated. But clearly education and the schools need to be renovated, to be made new again, but not in the sense of returning them to an earlier condition.

If renovation has only a past, and innovation only an ephemeral future, what of the present? The present belongs to reform.

Reform is the activity which links the past and the future, it is the ratio between the past and the future, and, in that sense, it is synonymous with intelligence. Reform is intelligence, the human mediation between various elements in the social and physical environment, the process of interaction in an insistent present. Reform, like intelligence, is not relevant, it is relevance, and it signifies whatever continuity our lives may have.

Of course, upon reflection, it might be assumed that I mean by reform what other people mean by planning. We have handed over our lives, our educational lives, to the planners and have not paused to reflect that the nature of planning itself might need development, that the planners might need learning. The conception of planning that we have inherited belonged to a time when the world was relatively static, when change did not occur, or, more accurately, when change took place so slowly that it could be treated as if it did not occur. This conception of planning saw its problems in terms of ends and means. Since planners were not the rulers, but were merely the hirelings, they had little to do with the formulation of ends. Goals were set, ends were announced, and the planner's main task was to devise the appropriate means for reaching the end. The whole activity was rather like going on a train journey, a tiresome business only justified by arrival at one's destination, at the terminal or depot.

Clearly, travel agents do perform a kind of planning, and, in that sense, they display a kind of rationality, but we cannot take this as the paradigm for educational planning and rationality now. The times have changed, and we must free ourselves from the notion that planning, rationality, is the devising of means to reach a preordained end, before the commencement of any activity. For us, planning cannot be prior to activity, it cannot be the precursor to life; it is the rational dimension of life as it is lived. It is concurrent and therefore it must be conceived as process.

Our language, with its commitment to the priority of nouns, always draws our attention to things, while what we need is a language in which the verbs can be subjects of sentences, hopefully excluding that pale apology, the gerund. To talk in terms of process is hard for us, and my sentences will appear overly complex and ponderous because of the nature of our language, but, in terms of our experience, what I mean is fairly simple. I decide to go to Pugwash, and, since there is neither bus nor train service, I am quick to decide that I shall drive. At once, end and means are determined, and by following the structure of the terrain, along the correct roads, I shall achieve my end. My success is dependent upon whether or not I reach Pugwash. Nothing else will do. Evaluation is absolute.

Contrast this with the situation in which I observe that, although there is snow on the ground, the sun has suddenly appeared. I am attracted outside and am immediately struck with the freshness of the air and the blueness of the clearing sky. I explore a little and start walking away from the house, pass the parked car with only a momentary thought of using it, and see children going down the hill on sleds. Maybe I should join them, or perhaps I could use my bicycle, which would be more dignified as long as I did not fall off . . .

In this latter case, there is no preconceived end, there is only the process to be enjoyed. As I act and interact, more possibilities become available to me, and so I undergo an education with respect to my goals which in turn become new means for further possible goals. In fact, the whole conception of ends and means becomes meaningless, as soon as I accept the process as having validity in itself.

Planning of the former kind has been extended and we can now plan to go to the moon and actually do it; we can plan to visit Venus, Mars, and maybe Jupiter or Saturn. Although these excursions involve a great deal of technical know-how, they do not involve the learning difficulty which goes with the abolition of poverty, let us say. This requires learning of a high order because there is a new goal, and because the process of fulfilling the goal threatens the habits of social thought current in our society. It is strange, but going to the moon does not.

Educational reform has been mistakenly conceived on the travel model. Better education has been thought to come from longer journeys, as it were–bigger buildings, larger groups, higher standards, technicolour textbooks, and more precise (but still preconceived) goals. Planning has been carried on accordingly, and there are shelves of reports and recommendations gradually accumulating dust, while the problems of education remain virtually untouched.

Reform will come about when we accept the challenge of living as process, when planning is the heart of the educational activity itself and not the precursor to it. This marks, in its own way, a revolution in thought as profound as that inaugurated by Copernicus or Freud, for it is the next step in the development of a democratic society in which our institutions will be judged by the extent to which they contribute to the learning of their members. Learning can no longer be maintained if all it does is to turn people into instruments of others' purposes; new goals are there for the creation, and the new learning deals with goals, purposes, and values which are now rigorously excluded from education.

This may only be another way of saying that learning is not a preparation for life but is the living part of life itself. The reality of reform consists in the maintained and increased ability of human individuals and human groups and structures to preserve themselves by changing. The indictment of our educational systems is that they have been unable to learn, they have not been self-educating; the indictment of our educational leaders is that they have turned away from the responsibility of learning and have sought to impose change upon others. *Plus ça change, plus c'est la même chose.* The indictment of ourselves is that we have allowed this to happen and have been too willing to let others set our goals, while we have complained about their tyranny. Perhaps reform is only possible among free people.

JOHN BREMER   *Commissioner of Education, British Columbia*

Introduction

Education, as Edmund Wilson put it, is the last hope of the liberal in all periods. In Canada, the 1960s provided a classic example of this maxim. Education, we were told, was the keystone of the entire social structure. Like women's liberation or ecology today, it seemed to permeate all other political and social issues. Education was a major growth industry, became the largest single budget-item in the public sector, and would produce, so we were assured, everything from everlasting economic prosperity to complete sexual fulfillment.

Of recent years, however, its stock has been declining. Education does not now seem to be the answer for every problem modern society faces. Indeed, the school system has come under increasing attack as being a major force in perpetuating those very inequities which it was supposed to eliminate. In short, having failed to satisfy the exaggerated expectations created by its promoters, education is now enjoying an excess of abuse for its considerable short-comings.

Perhaps we should let education fade back into a decent obscurity. Before we do so, however, it is worth pausing to consider the phenomenon of educational boom and bust over the past decade or so. How were the fundamental questions about social reform so easily swept aside in the rush of enthusiasm for this panacea? Why was the notion that the traditional concerns of the left were irrelevant and dated so widely accepted? As one of the editors of *This Magazine is About Schools* acknowledges, most people involved in educational reform–either in the counterculture or working within the system–suffered from the "mistaken idea that society was more open than it is, that power was not as entrenched as it is, and that the position of youth was very much removed from any control by the central parts of the society like the production system or the communications system." But, as is now painfully clear again, it is economic and fiscal policy which provides employment, not better job training in schools; redistribution of resources and wealth which eliminates the poverty-cycle, not improved inner-city school programs.

Though educational reform, as is now clear, is no substitute for fundamental social measures, that is not to say that it cannot play an important supporting and complementary role. It is essential, therefore, for those concerned about this relationship to examine the period just past, to ask what mistakes were made, and to begin to speculate about more realistic and fruitful approaches for the future. Despite the calls for de-schooling society, organized educational systems seem unlikely to disappear entirely, though their character and functions may change substantially. There remains every reason to make these systems, which touch almost everyone's life directly and over a long period of time, more humane, diverse, accessible, and responsive than they are or have been.

For these reasons, the editors of the *Canadian Forum* felt that an assessment of the significance of all the expenditure, reorganization, and change of the 1960s was opportune. A number of writers were invited to comment on specific themes—the traditions and growth of Canadian universities, federal-provincial relations, teacher education, Canadian Studies, and the development of community involvement in the schools. Several other authors were asked to survey the situation in their province or region across the country.

Though far from a complete inventory of the state of Canadian education in 1972 this collection does convey something of the current atmosphere of disenchantment and skepticism. Almost without exception the contributors seem to doubt the efficacy of many of the educational policies and "innovations" which characterize the last decade and to conclude that the general influence of educational reform is much more limited than we have supposed.

In his article, "Class, Bureaucracy, and the Schools," Michael Katz draws upon both American and Canadian sources to present a lucid analysis of the ideology and objectives of the public educational system. His exploration of the nature of educational reform and its relationship to broader issues of social policy provides an appropriate basis from which to read the rest of this collection.

To adapt the analogy Katz uses, if we think of the educational system as a room in a house, we have just emerged from a period during which we filled that room with an assortment of interesting and expensive pieces of furniture and accessories and spent a great deal of time and energy moving them about. Without really altering the structure of the room, we have redecorated it several times and have even built one or two additions to it. But we have tended to ignore the overall state of the house itself and the connections between its structure and that of the room.

We are moving into a period of great uncertainty and conflicting pressures in Canadian education. Against a backdrop of financial retrenchment and recorded priorities in the public sector, demands are heard that education be at once more effective, more continuous, and more available. The new policy directions for the 1970s are not yet clear. If, however, we hope to make education a more significant factor in general social reform during this decade than it was in the last, we must give serious attention to the problems and questions raised in this collection.

DOUGLAS MYERS

Class, Bureaucracy and Schools

Michael B. Katz

Not long ago I began a review of an American anthology
with an anecdote, which I later incorporated into a book
that attempts an historical social criticism of American education. That anecdote serves as a particularly fitting epigram
for this article:

> Seven poor mothers, disgusted with the treatment of their
> children in schools for slow learners, began a little school
> of their own. Located in a vacant slum house, it had ten
> children taught by four undergraduates from a local
> university. When it came time to elect members for the
> city school board, the mothers decided that one of their
> number stand. To plan the campaign they called on volun-
> teers from the university and from a political party. At
> campaign meetings in the schoolhouse, the mothers sat
> on one side of the room, projecting anger at a school
> system that, they felt, ignored and insulted them and their
> children. On the other side sat the outsiders, dressed
> mostly in casual clothes, with longish hair, who saw in the
> mothers an indigenous community movement representing
> educational radicalism and participatory democracy. Press-
> ed by the outsiders, the mothers offered personal stories
> of educational injustice, but very few specific educational
> objectives. When the candidate did adopt a platform, she
> advocated the reintroduction of report cards and corporal
> punishment; she opposed sex education.

Most readers have assumed that the contemporary incident

just described took place in an American city, and most people apparently consider it a fair representation of the dilemma posed by the gap between the aspirations of poor people and the educational radicals who come to help them. In fact, the incident occurred in Canada.

The ability of people on both sides of the border to identify with this situation highlights some important similarities in the dimensions of the educational problem in both countries and in the educational reform movement which has surfaced across the continent – indeed, in some respects across much of the world. As an historian I see a connection between the way in which public education began, its subsequent pattern of development and the contemporary educational crisis. Thus, any adequate discussion of that crisis and its cure must include some comprehension of its origins.

Unfortunately, the pietistic educational historians of earlier generations have left us with a singularly useless, as well as misleading, version of the educational past in both Canada and the United States. We are asked to believe a tale of sacrifice, heroism and triumph through which the contemporary public school came into existence as the great achievement of Western political culture. We are asked to believe in the essentially beneficent, egalitarian and ameliorating influence that public education has exercised in our societies for the past century. It is a story that simply does not fit the inadequacies of public education as we have come to know them in recent years.

In both Canada and the United States the work of a new generation of historians is beginning to revise fundamentally our understanding of how education came to be as it really is. It is as part of that effort to provide a social history of education at once scholarly and meaningful that my own writing has taken shape. The conclusion to which ten years of study and research in this field have led me is that there are now, and always have been, clear and systematic connections between the class biases of school systems and their bureaucratic structures. I shall elaborate that point of view, briefly, in the rest of this article.

Let me make it clear at the outset that the interpretation I wish to present was originally formulated with direct reference to American education. It seems to me worth setting out its main outlines in that context for two reasons: first, that many of the contours of the story of the development of public education are similar in both countries, and, secondly, that the argument acquires particular force when it can be demonstrated that its main features hold, even when the important and critical national distinctions have been set aside. Canadian and American educational practices have always reflected and reinforced the inequities of the social systems of which they are a part. In the last analysis it is the similarity in those inequities that has sustained a similarity in educational structure.

*   *   *

The basic structure of American education had been fixed by about 1880; it has not altered, fundamentally, since that time. That proposition, which I advance as the basis of this interpretation, poses five problems, four of them historical and one contemporary. The problems are these: first, did anyone propose alternatives to the structure that emerged? Second, was the establishment of that structure, regardless of alternative proposals, somehow "inevitable"? Third, what have been the interconnections between the major dimensions of that structure, or between its shape, its purpose and its function? Fourth, why has this structure remained so impermeable to reformist thrusts? And, fifth, what is the moral of this structure's history for contemporary reform, or, must structural change precede "educational" change?

First of all the proposition itself: the basic structure of American education had been fixed by 1880. Acceptance of that assertion rests, quite obviously, upon one's conception of basic structure. I mean by the phrase that American education had the following characteristics: it was universal, tax-supported, free, compulsory, bureaucratic, class-biased and racist. By 1880 those features all marked public educational systems in some places, most notably the Northeast. Before long they diffused themselves throughout the country, generally accompanying urban growth.

It would be tedious to recite all the evidence which bears on this proposition. In brief, when I say that the school system had become bureaucratic I mean that it had assumed, quite literally, those characteristics which sociologists would generally agree mark bureaucracy; for instance, hierarchy, division of function, specialization, precision, continuity, rule-following and discretion.

Public schools have always represented conservative social forces expressing and reflecting the aspirations, the fears and the interests of the more affluent members of communities; this is what I mean by class bias. In large measure the founding of public systems of education represented the attempt of the "better people" to do something to the rest. For the most part that meant the inculcation of attitudes and habits thought necessary to upright and orderly behaviour. In one form or another training in behaviour and belief has always been more important to people in control of schools than the development of intellectual skills. Although official educational rhetoric has proclaimed the schools agencies of upward mobility for the children of the poor, in fact they have more often protected the status of the well-to-do. The high school serves as a prime example here. Contrary to the predictions of its founders, relatively few poor children attended high schools during the first several decades of their existence. High schools helped the children of the middle class into white-collar jobs, while everyone, including the poor, paid the bills.

The racism inherent in public education relates closely to its class bias. I call racist an attitude which considers one group of people as essentially different from and inferior to another in some basic and virtually unchangeable way. This was the reformist perception of the urban poor, especially of Irish immigrants and their children, in the mid-nineteenth century at the time when public educational systems began. It was to civilize these poor, thereby preserving law, order and morality, that schools were thought by many people to be necessary. By embodying this attitude toward the poor into new institutions, public educational systems started with racism at their core.

The other characteristics of educational structure are even more easily apparent. By the late nineteenth century in areas that had public school systems virtually everybody went to school for some period of time. Schools had been supported by taxes for a long while, and taxes covered their extensions, like high schools which, despite some grumblings, remained as free as the rest of the system. For the contest for free schools had been fought and won earlier in the century. Finally, in Massachusetts compulsion had been law for almost thirty years in 1880, and it too, as we all know, diffused throughout the country.

It would seem unnecessary to labour the point that these characteristics have persisted. Education has become ever more universal, waves of attendance spreading upward from the common, through the high school and soon, it would seem, about to engulf the college. At the same time the public has assumed progressively larger educational burdens, paying for the new universality of higher levels with public money. Compulsion crept upward through age sixteen, and there are those who would extend it even now. Whether seeking its extension or not, compulsion, a once radical proposition, has been thoroughly accepted. It is now a reflex, a habit, and the burden of radical innovation has fallen to those who would attack it.

Bureaucracy remains the fundamental organizational form, as the reform movement of the last few years has made abundantly clear. It is the most striking feature of the educational landscape. As if by some biological process like the automatic division of cells, the bureaucratic elements present in 1875 continued to divide and multiply, and there is, insofar as I can tell, no sign whatsoever that the process has ceased. Similarly, contemporary reformers have made us painfully aware of the class and race biases of public education. These range from the purposes that education is supposed to serve, to the attitude of teachers, to the actual functioning of school systems which continue to secure differential advantage to the children of the affluent.

Thus it seems to me valid to argue that the structure of American education had been fixed by 1880 and that it has not changed substantially since that time. It is true that there have been important innovations; I do not want to deny that point. Certainly, the kindergarten, vocational education, guidance, testing and the new curricula, to name but a few of the most obvious, have all made differences. But they have not touched the structural features that I have described. It is, to use a very rough metaphor, as if the characteristics which I have noted form the walls of a box within which other sorts of changes have taken place. The box is filled with objects which can be moved around and rearranged, but the walls themselves remain solid. It is moreover the case, if I may extend this image for a moment, that only objects which fit can be put inside the box. Thus there is a congruence between the purposes and functioning of the innovations that have entered the schools themselves and the structural basis of the educational system.

*　　*　　*

This discussion should by now have made evident the meaning of the problems that I stated briefly at the outset of this discussion. To take the first: did anyone propose alternatives to the structure that emerged? Historians too easily have conceived of educational history in simple moralistic terms: there were the good men, reformers of vision, dedication and courage, who proposed in embryo the school system we have now. They were opposed by selfish, narrow-minded bigots interested in saving money and keeping the working classes down. We know that this is nonsense because we live with the unhappy results of those early proposals and because we find it hard today to accept simple and one-sided explanations of human behaviour. But we must, as well, reject this picture because of its constriction of historical vision. We must not accept the notion that there was one proposal around which the arguments revolved. To the contrary, in the first half of the nineteenth century four different proposals, four alternative modes of organizing public education, competed for acceptance in the United States.

Two points about those alternatives are worth emphasizing. First, each proposal – I call them paternalistic voluntarism, corporate voluntarism, democratic localism and incipient bureaucracy – rested on a distinct and identifiable set of social values, and the competition among them reflected and expressed wider value conflicts within society, as the Ocean-Hill Brownsville case or discussions of community control and decentralization do today. Second, they were real alternatives; examples of each did in fact exist. The one that emerged victorious was incipient bureaucracy which, as the model championed by the so-called educational revivalists, soon lost its incipient qualities.

The second problem is largely one of causation, Why did bureaucracy win? Was it somehow "inevitable"? This is a question of some importance for social theory as well as for historical inquiry. One implication of much modern social science, it seems to me, perhaps naively, is in fact that bureaucracy *is* inevitable. Given a complex, technological society and a complicated and massive social task, like universal schooling, there is no other rational way of proceeding. Bureaucracy is neither good nor bad in this point of view. It is a necessity; the alternative is chaos and anarchy. If the logic of this point of view is accepted, then reform directed against the notion and fact of bureaucracy is at best romantic and, in any case, useless. It is better to accept the reality and permanency of bureaucracies and to humanize their operations.

But if bureaucracy in education was inevitable, it did not seem so to some men who lived at the time of its creation in the United States. This is one moral of the story of alternative proposals. Some men at different points in time, in the 19th century and today, have been able to conceive of ways other than bureaucracy for managing the affairs of modern society. It is thus difficult to accept bureaucracy as the only way in which social tasks can be carried out.

In fact, on closer inspection, it would seem that bureaucracy is inevitable only when men confront certain tasks with particular social values and priorities. In other words, it is not industrialization that makes bureaucracy inevitable but the combination of industrialization and particular values. If efficiency is valued more than responsiveness, if order is valued more than participation, if uniformity is more important than individuality, if disorder is feared: if all these attitudes dominate the minds of men in industrial settings, then, indeed, bureaucracy is the only form of organization to which they can turn. Bureaucracy, in that circumstance, is inevitable. It is because of the mix of setting and priorities, not because of the setting alone, that we have bureaucracy as the dominant form of social organization.

This conclusion suggests answers to the third problem that I raised: the interconnections between the dimensions of educational structure or, as we now might phrase the question, between bureaucracy and social class. We know that education is bureaucratically organized. We know that it expresses class bias in its purposes, attitudes and functions. Are these two features independent, at least in their origins if not in their present form? The answer to that question, if my analysis is correct, is no. Bureaucracy came about because men confronted particular kinds of social problems with particular social values. Those values, some of which I have indicated above, are class values. Modern bureaucracy is a bourgeois invention: it represents a crystallization of bourgeois social attitudes.

To the founders of school systems educational purposes and structures were clearly interrelated. Early school promoters understood that part of the message they wished transmitted, the attitudes they wished formed, would inhere in the structural arrangements themselves rather than in explicit, didactic procedures. What they did not admit, though they must have realized it, was that structural elements of educational systems, like high schools, so apparently equitable and favourable to the poor, would in fact give differential advantage to the affluent and their children, thereby reinforcing rather than altering existing patterns of social structure. Through bureaucracy the myth of equal opportunity has been fostered while the amount of social mobility has been, in fact, strictly regulated.

The relationships between industrialization, bureaucracy, social class and social values can be combined into a more formal statement:namely, that one function of social organizations is to mediate between social change and social values. It is no accident that public education emerged in the nineteenth century along with modern pedagogy, modern psychiatric treatment, reform schools and mass-production. It was a time when the creation of institutions preoccupied the minds of men. That is because it was a period, as well, of intensive social change, the era of industrialization. My thesis – really a hunch at this juncture – is that industrialization, by disrupting the multi-purpose household, created the need for new organizations to stand between social problems and changes, on the one hand, and social values and priorities on the other. Organizations replaced the household as the mediators within society. As such they became the focus of values, attitudes, belief, of class interest and aspiration; men brought to their creation their visions of the good life and the good society, and they embodied those visions in the prosaic details of organizational structure and operation. That is why it is incorrect to view any form of social organization, including bureaucracy, as a disembodied neutral shell in which activities take place. Neither the relationships of social class nor bureaucracy to public education can be understood properly and fully without reference to each other.

* * *

Once more the analysis of the preceding problem provides

clues to the one that follows, in this case, why has the structure of American education remained so impermeable to reformist thrusts? Part of the answer, of course, is that the structure serves powerful interests. It serves the interests of the educators by providing career-lines and regulating entry. It serves the interests of affluent groups by working in favour of their children and giving them a disproportionate share of public funds. For those who control the system there has been no point in making fundamental structural alterations.

That is one reason why the system has remained unreformed. The other is that very few people, until now, have seriously tried to change it. The reforms that have been proposed at various times, and frequently even enacted, consist generally of moving around the objects in the box, to return to my earlier image. I include in this description the reformers of the progressive period of the late nineteenth and early twentieth century. We must look beyond the rhetoric of child-liberation and curricular innovation that they articulated and see, for one thing, that they did not attack or even consider very much the structure of the school system; they took for granted, as given, the characteristics which I have suggested give it definition. More than that, it is possible to see within their theory, including especially that of Dewey and Jane Addams, subtle attempts to substitute new forms of social control for old ones, to instil an essentially conformist and group-oriented set of attitudes and behaviours profoundly congruent with industrial values. If their proposals had succeeded, and for the most part they did not, the unintended consequence might well have been to make men content with their lot, to substitute for an older, competitive individualism a new and more appropriate social myth stressing the importance of the productive worker to the welfare of society.

But educational theorists formed only one strand of the educational reform movement of the period. Without discussing that movement in any detail, it is important to indicate, first, that its most characteristic activity was probably the attempt to change the governing structure of city educational systems by substituting the control of an elite, small central school committee for the large, socially more heterogeneous and allegedly corrupt ward-based ones that existed in most places. As such it was part of a larger municipal reform movement whose class relations a number of American historians have discussed ably in the last few years. Second, a number of innovations were quite consistent with the structure and tenor of education as it then existed. Vocational education, the testing movement and guidance can be put in a somewhat cynical perspective as elaborations and refinements of bureaucracy, and as instruments of social regulation necessary to preserve the class relations within school systems whose clientele was expanding rapidly in numbers and, at the secondary level, in social diversity. Slightly cynical though that perspective may be, it nonetheless expresses the consequences, if not the conscious intent, of a number of major innovations.

My point is very simply that reform has generally either ignored the structural components of educational systems or reinforced them. It has not attacked those structures; it has not tried to knock down the walls of the box instead of tinkering with what is inside. I believe that the main outlines of this interpretation hold true for Canada as well as the United States. Certainly my work in the history of Canadian education over the past half dozen years convinces me that the interrelationships among bureaucracy, class and education are no less prominent, entrenched, or harmful in Ontario than in Massachusetts.

There are, of course, critical historical and contemporary differences between education in the two places, but these do not alter the similarities in what I have termed basic structure. For instance, competing models of educational organization in Upper Canada in the early and mid nineteenth century must be conceptualized in a rather different fashion. Any adequate formulation must take into account, at the very least, the successful establishment of a separate, tax-supported and religiously based school system. But the difference in the conceptualization does not alter the broader point that different organizational models, embodying different value systems, competed in each country.

Nor does it alter the conservative and class-oriented nature of the arguments of leading proponents of public schooling in Upper Canada, and the similarity of their aspirations and objectives to those of their counterparts in the United States. The scorn with which schoolmen regarded the poor and the desire to ensure social order at the heart of educational innovation are, alas, unmistakable in Canadian as well as American writing. (A number of articles in a recent issue of the *History of Education Quarterly* devoted to Canadian education provide ample corroboration of this.)

It is probably the case that the ideology of educational promotion in the nineteenth century was rather less egalitarian in Canada than in the United States. The promotion of social mobility and the mixing of social classes in common schools, while frequent themes, were put less stridently by Egerton Ryerson than by Horace Mann. Yet, rhetorical nuances aside, the way in which the school systems that both men promoted served to reinforce existing social structures was not all that different.

Certainly, though, Horace Mann and other American state superintendents must have envied the degree of centralization that Ryerson and his successors achieved. Less hampered by an ideological defence of localism, the bureaucratic model could emerge in purer form in Ontario than in most places in America. This success of centralism cuts two ways: few, if any, contemporary differences strike the American observer of education in urban Ontario quite so immediately as the relative lack of wide discrepancies between schools in city and suburb. Divergence in standard does exist, but there is nothing comparable to the gap between Harlem and Scarsdale or between Roxbury and Newton. From a different perspective, it has probably been somewhat more difficult for grass-roots innovation to begin in Canadian than in American schools, for the weight of centralism, historically, has made local experiment difficult.

Nonetheless, the main lines of innovation, even their timing, have been relatively similar, at least in Ontario, to what was happening in the United States. What is important is that, despite the national differences that did exist, reform in Canada also represented moving around the furniture in a box whose walls had been firmly and unshakably built.

* * *

The crisis in American education has been part of the black/white racial crisis, both North and South. For this reason it is possible to maintain a degree of complacency about the lack of class and racial bias in Canadian schools, especially when they remain untorn by strife expressing itself quite literally as rebellion both inside and outside of the classroom. But the aura of gentility that still clings to Canadian education should not obscure the fact that Canadian schools serve the poor no better than American ones, and that the attitudes of Canadian schoolmen may remain no less condescending, biased and, even, implicitly racist than those of many of their counterparts in the United States. I was made memorably conscious of this when I heard a high official of a Canadian school system discussing the problem of education in the inner city, particularly that of poor immigrant children. Referring to an article by an American psychologist, Arthur Jensen, which has been widely if simplistically taken to mean that Negroes are genetically less intelligent than whites, this school official claimed, "of course, Jensen has told us all about them," meaning the poor immigrant children for whose education he is responsible.

Thus we return to the seven poor mothers in a Canadian slum. They could be taken as American because in both places they and their children would be the casualties of an educational bureaucracy which has never served them well. In both places that bureaucracy, in fact, cannot serve them properly because its very form is the crystallization of a set of attitudes and purposes which work against their best interests. In other words, it is not possible to alter the purposes, biases and actual functioning of schools without at the same time changing, radically, the structures through which they are organized and controlled. Forms of organizational structure are not and cannot be neutral. To change educational outcomes it is necessary, at the same time, to change educational structures.

But that, of course, is a very complex task. Moreover, the box which is the educational system exists within a larger box, which is the society that created it. And that society, in turn, rests on the perpetuation of gross inequalities in the distribution of power and resources. For this reason there can be no meaningful educational reform which is not at the same time part of a broader effort to alter the inequities which Canadian and American schools have been designed to sustain.

Intellectual Tradition and Academic Colonialism

D. L. Davies

-I-

In the recent debate on the Canadianization of universities, the emphasis has been placed on the domination of particular institutions and disciplines by foreign – and in particular U.S. – academics. What has not received much attention is how an indigenous intellectual tradition is formed, notably in a situation where the political and economic parameters are both colonial and provincial. In other words, the thrust of the Canadianization campaign up to now has been negative: it has demonstrated the ways that Canadian higher education has progressively been influenced, and perhaps been controlled by U.S. personnel and institutional precedents. It has not offered much of a solution on how something that is neither U.S. nor British nor French might emerge: the only guidelines relate to Canadian 'content', courses in the literature, history, economics, sociology or politics of Canada. But of course Canadian topics might be taught within theoretical frameworks that are totally 'foreign', and a tradition might be claimed as 'Canadian' which is in fact simply an earlier colonial import.

I would therefore like to approach the crisis of the present direction of higher education in English Canada by focusing on the problems of creating and developing an intellectual culture. Most of my examples will refer to the humanities and social sciences (mainly because I am most at home with them), though much of what I have to say is also applicable to the natural sciences. But first I ought to say what I mean by 'culture', by 'intellectual' and by the two terms taken together.

My definitions derive in large measure from an American poet who took British citizenship, a Czech political scientist who taught in Britain and the U.S.A., and an English social philosopher (with a 'European' intellectual orientation) who holds Canadian citizenship. These international and inter-disciplinary backgrounds are not accidental: I want to stress throughout this essay the importance of internationalism in creating the orientation of intellectual pursuits. But first the definitions.

In his *Notes towards the Definition of Culture*, T. S. Eliot states that:

> . . . . . . *the culture of the individual cannot be isolated from that of the group, and the culture of the group cannot be abstracted from that of the whole society; and our notion of 'perfection' must take all three senses of 'culture' into account at once. Nor does it follow that in a society, of whatever grade of culture, the groups concerned with each activity will be distinct and exclusive: on the contrary, it is only by an overlapping and sharing of interests, by participation and mutual appreciation, that the cohesion necessary for culture can obtain. A religion requires not only a body of priests who know what they are doing, but a body of worshippers who know what is being done.*

Eliot's definitions presuppose a symbiotic relationship between the individual, the group and the totality: culture is partial and comprehensive, at one level simply the ways that people make sense of their daily lives, and at another, "that which makes life worth living." In a society created by immigration, conquest, and economic colonialism, the dominant symbols that people use to make sense will necessarily be fragmentary. Some symbols will come from the superimposed political and economic institutions (which may be external) and some from the ongoing day-to-day institutions that have the most immediate meaning for social relationships. Biculturalism and bilingualism, coupled with wide physical distances and political federalism, necessarily increase the chances of cultural fragmentation, though possibly they also increase the chances of cultural domination by those who are closest to the controlling mechanisms (a theme which runs through John Porter's *Vertical Mosaic*). In particular, they decrease the chances of there existing an intellectual tradition which can act as the focal point for national political, social or economic debate. The position of the intellectual in a society which has few explicit cultural parameters is wholly ambiguous. But what is an 'intellectual'?

In a penetrating essay on "Ideas, Intellectuals and Structures of Dissent" (in Philip Fieff, ed., *On Intellectuals*, 1970) the late Peter Nettl argued that the term intellectual makes little sense if we reduce it to the role-categories of 'academic', 'scientist' and the like: all we are talking about here are occupations which are only one aspect of the situation. Nettl begins by accepting Edgar Morin's definition:

> *The intellectual emerges from a cultural base and with a socio-political role (cultural in this sense is defined as a self-conscious concern with cultural dimensions). . . Thus the intellectual can be defined from a triple set of dimensions*: (*i*) *a profession that is culturally validated,* (*ii*) *a role that is socio-political, (iii) a consciousness that relates to universals.* (Morin, "Intellectuals: critique du mythe et mythe de la critique", *Arguments* Vol IV, No 20, Oct 1960, p. 35).

The first point stresses that the intellectual must have an audience which recognizes that what he has to say is important for matters of cultural concern; the second that his role in society is not simply that of a transmitter of a cultural heritage or the manufacturer of ideas but is based on a conception of social action; the third that his search is not for particularities but for generalizable laws. Nettl's essay is concerned mainly with exploring the relationship between intellectuals and social movements and, in particular, movements of political dissent. He argues that not only is intellectual creativity derived from dissent (whether or not the intellectuals were for or against the particular dissenting ideology) but that the future of academic freedom depends on social scientists and more particularly scientists in maintaining the momentum of dissent.

So the intellectual is more than an academic, and indeed may not be an academic at all. In particular he is a man who has an audience which recognises that what he has to say is worth listening to because it affects its culture (whether individual, group or national), he recognizes the social and political significance of his ideas for action and he is not content to reduce his thinking to the particularities of the situation or society in which he finds himself: his *conscience*, to use the French term, "suggests a universalization of awareness as well as of feeling, thus covering both values and cognition. *Conscience* is therefore to be contrasted not only with particularism as a system of thought but also with professionalism as a social category". (Nettl, p. 90)

But in contemporary society the professionalization and institutionalization of knowledge have made this intellectual stance difficult to cultivate. The audience for the intellectual is either a group of categorized students or fellow 'professionals'; the socio-political role is defined for him by federal or provincial assemblies or by the labelling process of the mass media; while the 'universals' are either reduced to the particularism of a specific discipline or subsection of a discipline, or else are blanket ideologies which assume most of what the academic should be questioning. In such a situation the task of the intellectual is a difficult one. Discussing sociology John O'Neill (in *Sociology as a Skin Trade*, to be reviewed in a later issue of the *Forum*) suggests the critical task:

Sociology . . . . promises to give back to the people what it takes from them. This is true of all culture but sociology

more than any other discipline promises to make this a
practical truth. This is not to say that sociology does not
need the other sciences. On the contrary, it presupposes
other physical and social sciences. But it has its own task
in the need to articulate the connections between individual
experience and the transvaluation of human sensibilities
worked by the institutional settings of technology, science
and politics. . . This means that the rhetoric of scientism
in sociology as well as humanism must be tested against
the commonsense relevance of everyday life.

The development of an intellectual culture is simply the
establishment of this symbiotic relationship. I would like to
suggest the obstacles and possibilities in contemporary
Canada.

-II-

The critical issue in the development of universities *every-
where* is that rarely are they the centres of creative, innovative research and thinking without being dependent on
external stimulation. Certainly they employ people who are
creative and innovative, but only in a few cases can it be
shown that universities themselves have contributed more
than facilities towards intellectual creativity. Traditionally
universities are parasitic. They employ professors whose
creativity has been fostered in non-academic milieux, or at
least a different academic milieu (here Canada is particuarly
vulnerable). They study literature, painting, people, institutions, things which have their being outside the university.
Creativity has as its audience not the regimented professionals of a discipline, or the promotion or tenure committees
of a particular university, nor even the students packaged
into absurd categories of honours, general or graduate, but
audiences which are external. No university can claim credit
for fostering Dada or Surrealism, Freud or James Joyce,
George Lukacs or Arthur Koestler, Marx or Engels, Walter
Benjamin or Edmund Wilson, Neitzsche or Pascal, or even

Max Weber. In some cases the universities can congratulate themselves for housing them or even giving them laboratories and students for a few years but rarely for providing more than a negative catalyst for their creativity. What universities do is to narrow down, plagiarize or otherwise traduce this creativity. If they see themselves as passing on or transmitting a cultural heritage it is done through the commodity-relations of students to professor, courses to credits, ideology to disciplinary professionalism.

Why then bother about Canadian universities? Why should they succeed where others have failed? To put the question this way is to show the extent to which I have over-stated my argument, and the extent to which universities themselves have fostered a self-image they cannot possibly live up to and have created expectations which they cannot fulfil. Universities are simply part of a cultural matrix. They can give a particular definition to part of a culture, but they do not create it. In most respects they are no better or worse than the societies of which they are a part. But if our task is to examine how intellectual cultures can grow, then the universities are an integral part of the facilities, the thought processes, and the *ambience* within which ideas flourish, socio-political roles are defined and the orientations towards universals are arrived at. To examine our universities, therefore, is to commence an examination of what an indigenous, universalistic and critical culture requires for survival and growth.

Superficially, Canadian higher education represents a mélange of different styles derived from across the world: French, English, Scottish, u.s., and even traces of German and Belgian. It might be pointed out (naively) that Queens and Dalhousie are Scots foundations, Laval French, ubc and McGill English, York, Western Ontario and Simon Fraser American, and the proposed University of Ontario an improvement on Britain's Open University. In fact Queen's is now no more Scots than the University of Ottawa is like Louvain: what does make the difference is attitude of mind.

Canada has university structures which have evolved according to the exigencies of political, social and economic pressures (whatever the origins), but it preserves minds which are locked into other metropolitan cultures. Most economists, scientists, philosophers, sociologists, political scientists in Canada would never dream of writing articles for Canadian journals (in some cases because the journals are intellectually substandard or simply don't exist, but generally because their own intellectual orientations are external: one Ontario university classifies journals for its faculty according to international prominence and finds little room for Canadian journals in any of its rankings). As I shall argue later, to have an international forum is essential: what is distressing is that as Canadian education stands now it is not internationalist at all but rather consists of a series of intellectual ethnic ghettoes in which there is no debate *within* Canada that draws on this international richness. If Canadian universities represent in microcosm the multiculturalism of the wider society, they also have difficulty in drawing on this diverse intellectual experience to provide some interpretation that, as Nettl would have said, is culturally validated. That this need not be so is suggested by two examples derived from the pre-1960's.

In Toronto during the 1940's and 1950's the growth of a 'school' encompassing economic history, geography, literary criticism, anthropology and sociology is an indication of how an 'indigenous' tradition can be formed. Harold Innis, Edmund Carpenter, Marshall McLuhan, Northrop Frye and S. D. Clarke were not drawing on one metropolitan cultural tradition, but two at least. Both Chicago and Oxbridge were significant influences. Robert Park at one extreme, F. R. Leavis at the other. The critical issue, as far as I can see from a perusal of the writings of the central figures round the Innis school and the *Explorations* group, was that the focus was not on the problems of a discipline (there is nothing so arid in academic discourse as a group of men from one discipline talking to one another within the same basic assumptions), but on a substantive problem (communications) which was of critical significance to Canadian society but also had universalistic applications. The rich seam tapped by this school has not yet been mined by Canadian intellectuals.

But the University of Toronto became a large bureaucratic outfit concerned largely with the mass production of students and the cultivation of safe contractual and discipline-bounded research. As this is what most American universities are about anyway, it clearly could not compete. An intellectual birth was killed off. Historians specialized in embellishments of the early Innis work while ignoring the later *oeuvre;* S. D. Clarke packed his new sociology department with Amercians who specialized; Edmund Carpenter went away; and Marshall McLuhan did his own thing.

Another 'moment' in the development of a Canadian intellectual school can be seen in Quebec from the 1930's to the 1950's in the growth of sociology. One of the misconceptions in English Canada about intellectual life in Quebec is that it is 'French'. In fact, as any examination of Quebec sociological studies will show, the distinctive feature is that two sociological traditions – French and u.s. – were pitted against each other in an attempt to interpret Quebec society. One alone would not do: witness the early attempts at 'explaining' Quebec social change in terms of Robert Redfield's folk-urban continuum (episodes of which debate are found in Rioux and Martin's, *French-Canadian Society,* Toronto 1965). A further example is furnished by Guy Rocher in his *A General Introduction to Sociology* (Toronto, 1972) which, while not being an introduction to Quebec society, demonstrates the richness of a sociology that moves with ease in two cultures. Consequently sociology becomes less the replication of foreign styles of thought than the testing of concepts and ideas against the perceived and lived-in reality of Quebec life.

There are other examples, but two should suffice to show that academic intellectual cultures can be formed in a multicultural society which are more than the sum of the parts of the cultures. The obstacles to this development are in part due to the paths the universities themselves have chosen to travel, and in part to the provincial and federal structures within which they operate. I would like to consider this development by focusing first on changes in the universities themselves, before returning to the topic of an intellectual culture.

-III-

Examining universities as learning experiences involves tracing a style of thought which emerges out of the social structure that relates teacher to student. The Western Hemisphere provides three ideal types of such structures. The English system traditionally stressed the academic discipline as the focal point of all learning experience, though initially through Classics the discipline was itself interdisciplinary – involving a language, a philosophy, a literature, history as well as law and politics; thus the concept of discipline was in itself somewhat more broadly defined than in other countries. One of the features of this kind of education was that it gave the professor considerable power in determining what education was all about. The European (or Latin) system, of which Scotland was a variant, emphasized both the scope of knowledge, and the importance of an integrating discipline (usually philosophy, though the Russians were able to substitute Marxism-Leninism without much difficulty). Coupled with this was the even more hierarchical importance of the professor, though in this case his power came as much from the position of presiding over the integration of the package of subjects as from being a specialist. The student who survived was the one who made the *right* connections. The third type, the u.s., might be best described as a supermarket. Students chose courses, rather than subjects, thus the integration of knowledge was largely up to them. The disciplines, however, were rather narrowly defined and consisted of a greater division of labour between academics and teachers than in Europe. In this way it was possible to admit large numbers into the university while at the same time claiming that academic standards were being kept high. The student who chose the right (i.e. single-discipline) packages could move on to graduate school and become a 'specialist': the rest were put out to grass in commerce and industry.

Of course in each country there were exceptions to these generalizations, and they became more frequent as the twentieth century added more students and increased the quantity of knowledge available as well as accelerating the need to provide different forms of integration and new specialists for the market.But for our purposes the typology is useful as a beginning.

Most of the older universities in Canada started within the English, the Scots or the Latin traditions. But during the 1950's and more rapidly in the 1960's Canadian universities progressively adopted U.S. teaching structures and models for research. When they talked about creating departments of 'international stature' they meant that Canada should be able to attract scholars who produced Canadian equivalents of the Michigan surveys on voting behaviour or who could set up laboratories which accepted Skinnerian behavioural psychology as the premises for research. In teaching and the ordering of the curriculum they quickly abandoned the idea that undergraduate students should be given a basic core of subjects – a feature common to both the English and the Latin systems – and allowed them instead to take almost anything on the assumption that the student, in spite of the school system and the fact that most subjects were completely new, would himself be able to assemble a coherent package. Thus at one level (the subject-content of departments) the universities became absurdly specialist; at another (that of student choice of the curriculum) they looked generously interdisciplinary. In fact the specialization of professors when set against the generality of students' education created a hierarchy of specialists which excluded most students who, when confronted by a discipline, felt like Richard III, "come into this world scarce half made up." Inevitably undergraduate studies became the chore that professors had to perform in order to get on to the real thing – the initiation of graduate students into the sacred mysteries of a 'discipline'. The power of the foreign school of thought and of foreign-trained professors (mainly u.s.) was thus doubly-enforced. In graduate schools when students began to work out connections they were failed or put down by their professors for making the *wrong* connections. (For example in sociology, the social science discipline most affected by imperial models, all Canadian universities by 1970 had only graduated 20 ph.d.'s ever). If they passed it was because they had been successfully initiated into the rituals of a particular school of thought. I should hasten to add that I am not referring to the fact that many professors were foreign, though that is obviously a factor. In fact mentality is in many cases more important than country of origin. Irving Layton has written of a Canadian professor:

A native of Kingston, Ont.,
Went to Oxford, Eng.
Now even the English
Find their accents unmistakably colonial.

Much more serious than the branch-plant university is the branch-plant mind. Such a mind is not 'international' (any more than Canadian trade unions are international) but 'unmistakably colonial'.

The creation of new universities from the 1930's to the 1960's consisted, for the most part, of reinforcing these trends. The concept of the supermarket university in which undergraduates shopped around for cans labelled 'creative drama', the 'sociology of deviance' or the 'politics of ecology' became the norm. If, in some cases, it was fortunate that not all undergraduate students were being submitted totally to a system of thinking that was a closed shop because of the possibility of coming up with surrealistic combinations, on the other hand they often had little logical training to allow them to evaluate different disciplines or approaches. Canadian higher education reinforced the consumerism of the society: courses, like other commodities, could be chosen according to their apparent usefulness or packaging (a concept which the Ontario Wright Commission takes up and develops as a principle of education with crushing brutality: not even Marx could have imagined the extent to which the fetishism of commodities could be applied to ideas). For many students working through this kind of system, apart from the instrumental value of taking credits, the educational experience is totally meaningless. In this respect, at least, Ivan Illich is right. On the other hand if students *do* make sense of the various packages, they may well find that their knowledge exceeds that of their professors. In this sense Harold Taylor (in his book, *Students without Teachers,* 1970) may be right.

Thus the development of new universities was accompanied by the idea that 'skill' meant either the highly specialized (M.A.'s, PH.D.'s) or people with a general range of subjects whose minds would be sufficiently pliable to be employed by anyone anywhere (except, presumably, by universities). But there apparently existed a little discomfort that universities could be about something else than mass-produced students or the simple replication of U.S. discipline research. Two examples suggest the difficulties of such a realization. Simon Fraser is the most dramatic. Situated on the crest of Mount Burnaby, in an architectural setting which film producers have found ideal for a new version of Orwell's *1984,* it was to be the Canadian equivalent of Palo Alto, with aspects of Heidelberg, Sussex and Nanterre. In some cases disciplines were scrambled – Politics, Sociology, Anthropology; all behavioural studies – and both American and European intellectuals were hired, at some cost, to supervise operations. But its error was that of Karl Mannheim: to believe that intellectuals, detached from society and the rough-and-tumble of life, would be able to operate as twentieth-century equivalents of Plato's guardians. As the

PSA department showed, to pack a university with intellectual radicals, unless they are social eunuchs, was bound to raise questions about the university's purpose and the direction of the society in which it was located. Because Canada has no dominant intellectual culture, Simon Fraser failed, having no tradition to which it could appeal. (The CAUT defence of the radicals was based on completely unintellectual grounds, the preservation of the jobmarket status-quo). With its ex-CIA President, its subservience to the dictates of a huckstering provincial government and its inability to defend even liberal intellectual ideals, Simon Fraser sold Mannheim down the river. What it also showed was that it is possible to purchase foreign intellectuals at a price, but it is impossible to manufacture an intellectual culture.

But the scenario had been played out seven years earlier in Toronto. When York University was founded in 1962, the original idea was to create a living intellectual community in Glendon. (Glendon? Well at least Bayview is a less rarified social atmosphere than Burnaby Mountain.) Anyone with the stomach for such things can follow the saga of John Seeley versus Murray Ross in the pages of the *Toronto Star* through 1962. The essentials of the disagreement were between a California-type campus with many institutions and students, and a small, elite college with a self-conscious intellectual community. Seeley's intention was of filling an evident void in English-Canadian academic life by creating a Canadian Harvard-Oxbridge. He lost, and the university that emerged, though only remotely like California, was concerned with filling quite different gaps: adult education, bilingualism, curriculum innovation, interdisciplinary research, law reform, and the creative arts. It is too soon to say how successful it will be at these things (though Atkinson and Osgoode Hall Law School already look like providing permanent attacks on existing vested interests). But physically to set a university in the concrete wilderness of Downsview without adequate transport or social amenities, was perhaps the final indication of how little the government of Ontario took seriously the idea of a socially integrated intellectual community.

But the dimensions of an educational culture are not simply bounded by the availability of intellectuals and an established tradition of academic debate. They are also affected by audience, and by the existence (or absence) of a critically alert 'lay' public. The story that every Frenchman has read at least one book by Sartre may be a myth, but it does illuminate the difference between societies where ideas are taken as intrinsically important for everyday concerns and those where they are dismissed as ivory-tower nothings. Contrast the book review sections of the *Globe and Mail* with those of the London *Guardian* or *Times*, the *New York Times*, *Le Monde* or even *Le Devoir* to see what I mean: and here we are only staying with the minority audiences. The *Globe* has virtually no sense of a cultured, internationally aware public which would find Sartre or George Lukacs or André Malraux or the international avant-garde novelists or critics (let alone sociologists, political scientists or philosophers) remotely interesting. In a society which has so many immigrants from Europe and the Far East this is very surprising, doubly so when the Royal Ontario Museum can get itself an international reputation by taking its audiences seriously enough to build on their multicultured experiences *and* educate them.

Part of the problem is the conception of adult education as instrumental in, or related largely to, economic success. There have been attempts to cultivate a different relationship between universities and the public, but in general they have existed outside the main population centres. St. Francis Xavier, Memorial and the University of Saskatchewan are three where the idea of adult education contained something of the idea of social movement rather than the arid degree specialization that passes for 'extension' work in most universities. Unfortunately social work moralism and community development professionalism are replacing social movement, though St. Francis Xavier bravely soldiers on. The Ontario

Wright Commission Report proposal to coordinate adult education through the University of Ontario is perhaps the first sign in affluent Canada that a government is interested in taking the subject seriously. In spite of the crass consumerist philosophy underlying it, we must be thankful for small mercies. Beyond this, the rapport with society must surely take place outside the universities altogether, but I shall return to that in my conclusion.

The fundamental problem is that if academic knowledge is subdivided on rigid division-of-labour lines; if the only contact the public has with academic ideas is through the highly artificial course-credit system; if the main concern of provincial governments is with minimizing costs; and if the universities themselves see their tasks as being to reduce ideological conflict and keep their noses clean – then the prospects for the evolution of an intellectual culture are bleak.

-IV-

Similar problems emerge when we consider research policies. It is perhaps sufficient to consider three areas briefly.

As it stands now educational research is largely the prerogative of the provinces. This has meant progressively that the funding (some of it very generous) is used to answer direct policy questions: such things as the continuous search for new teaching techniques, curriculum innovations, costing systems and so on. The nature of this research comes very close to consultancy work. It is therefore hardly surprising that Canada has contributed very little to innovative thinking in education and why, in spite of such institutes as OISE, the sociology, psychology or politics of education in Canada is such a desert, in which *This Magazine is About Schools* appears as the only oasis. The implications of the funding policy are that it is difficult to have any research that does more than deal with minutiae. It is virtually impossible to do comparative research, even within Canada; statistics are poorly collected and generally unreliable, and almost no theory is generated.

In a different way Canada looks like killing non-policy research in the Third World too. The International Development Research Committee now has the monopoly on official Canadian research money going to the developing countries. So far IDRC has emphasized research which is strictly linked to practical questions and usually questions of some interest to the governments in the Third World. As other agencies now consider IDRC the main funding body for overseas research, it increasingly looks as if Canada will virtually cease to sponsor research which is (a) critical, (b) non-practical, (c) broadly theoretical, (d) linked to dissident elements in the particular societies. With the tendency in many developing countries to discourage critical, social scientific research, Canada, far from being liberal in its policy (i.e. by inviting the Third World countries to suggest their own research priorities), looks like becoming an ally for the existing political control systems. It's a strange form of aid.

But perhaps one of the strangest developments is within the universities themselves. Some years ago the President of a large Ontario university (which I keep anonymous to save it from embarrassment) established a Committee on Research involving Human Subjects, in some ways modelled on Medical Ethics committees which concern themselves with experimentation on human beings. The unique feature of this committee is that it also covers the social sciences. In these cases, however, the medical concern with unauthorized experimentation is reinterpreted as invasion of the privacy of the individual (usually interpreted as the practice of being a 'participant observer', or not revealing identity in research). Consequently the committee vets all projects which involve interviewing people, overhearing conversations, using police records and so on. The committee itself has a heavy legal bias, its secretary is a lawyer and a law professor is a semi-permanent consultant. To my knowledge cases which have given the committee some anxiety include examinations of criminal records, observations of homosexual behaviour, and the monitoring of calls to the police (the police responses were the objects of study, but the committee were worried that the public might not like to be overheard). Currently it is worried about the propriety of doing field research in New Guinea. It is interesting to speculate what the committee would do with a former student, Erving Goffman, the essence of whose research is precisely *not* to reveal his identity.

Of course the whole thing is nonsensical, but why does it exist? Obviously the university is not particularly concerned with the privacy of the individual, rather that it might find itself in court. The university is protecting itself, not the citizen. It therefore holds one profession (law) in higher estimation than the pursuit of knowledge. The issue has nothing to do with ethics or morality. The committee does not, for example, wrestle with such issues as the public right to know or even whether a professor has the right to requisition the work of one of his students and pass it off as his own.

In a conversation with the Commissar of the University's Ethics Squad, I raised the question of whether the university did not have a responsibility to the public as well as to the individual. The question was dismissed as 'fascist', the example given was Hitler's experimentation on individuals in the public interest. It was also argued that the public interest was being taken care of by the Ontario government: the universities had no business to meddle. In such circumstances it is idle to protest that Hitler was the head of the elected German government, that human experimentation and social research are not the same thing, or that abdicating all responsibility for critical thinking was precisely why Eichmann was put on trial. The legal mind and the liberal mind together in this case produced a bureaucratic monster. It is difficult to see that any of their activities have anything to do with intellectual concerns, except to suppress them.

This is not the whole picture, by any means, but they are straws in the wind. To create an intellectual culture we have to learn to fight provincial, federal and university bureaucracies. How can we do it?

-V-

Most industrial societies have modes of communication, political associations and the like which act as non-academic foci for intellectual creativity. Universities may be the employment centres for intellectuals, but they are rarely the creative centres. In the social sciences and humanities the interplay between social movement, technical and cultural changes, personal experiences and critical debate provides the dialectical moment for theoretical and creative shifts. Where this is not true – that is where the professors see the universities and their own professional or discipline identity as paramount – they demonstrate the similarity between the academic, the dentist or the undertaker: the mundane nature of their professional activity is camouflaged by the pomposity of etiquette and the cult of the ante-room. That one grain of methodological precision so carefully cultivated for a ph.d. thesis is decked out as the ultimate tree of knowledge. (For superb satirical accounts of this genus see E. P. Thompson, *Warwick University Ltd,* Penguin 1970, and John O'Neill's essay quoted above.)

Canada is, in most respects, no different from other societies, but there are two factors which do make a difference and which should concern anyone whose interest in academic knowledge and intellectual matters reaches beyond disciplinary professionalism and the mass production of creditworthy students. These are that a large percentage of teachers in higher education are foreign or foreign-trained, and that most of the creative milieux for intellectuals are also external Both of these have a common source: Canada's colonial status and in particular her colonial intellectual status. The attempt to manufacture an 'intellectual' tradition by importing foreign academics to an artificially created institution is just as much a mark of colonialism as the idea that only foreign conceptual frameworks have any validity. In such a context it is possible for Canadians to have scholars of international prominence without Canada herself benefiting from their presence. The real problem is the relation of this international expertise to the experiences, sensibilities and problems of Canada. The danger with the American penetration of Canadian academic life is that by the imposition of thought processes Canadians will indeed come to believe that knowledge-constructs superimposed on their society are in fact the interpretation of that society. The inevitable failure to produce anything with which Canadians identify is bound to produce Frankensteins on a par with the CBC's failure to get into the bigtime drama league with *Jalna* because it had not bothered to foster external Drama, not to speak of a resident Repertory company, before going for the tops. Intellectual traditions are not created or developed by instant gimmicks, but by the self-critical, cohesive effort of intellectuals themselves, over a long period of time, to create their own sense of movement. If they fail to do this, their bailiwick will be preëmpted by an imperialism of the mind in which the points of reference will always be a single external source.

Basically, there are three critical areas for advance: one relating to the ways that universities conceive of their teaching and staffing policies, one relating to provincial and federal funding policies for research, and the last to the attitudes that academics adopt to their audiences.

Internally, given that virtually all Canadian teaching and research operate on theoretical assumptions that have been derived from foreign work, it is imperative that universities do not confine themselves to maintaining a status quo in ideas. As mentioned earlier in relation to the early development of the social sciences at Laval and the University of Toronto, the most fruitful basis for an indigenous intellectual tradition in Canada (or, indeed, anywhere) is the confrontaton between at least two foreign schools of thought and at least two disciplines, all of them focusing on a substantive problem of importance to Canada and capable of universal applications. This means that we should not be afraid of foreign ideas, but welcome them as long as we are not welcoming only *one* country's exports. The polemic of Mathews and Steele is convincing as long as it tells us that we have been subject to only one foreign model: it stops short when it cannot advise us how we might do otherwise, except by restricting the appointment of Americans and teaching courses about Canada. If there is a Canadian intellectual tradition it is one which is interdisciplinary and focused on specific problems. To argue that because of the "exponential growth in information" we must all specialize and narrow our focus (the usual defence of the disciplinary hack) is an abdication of the responsibility of intellectuals and a guarantee that we will neither create anything nor break out of colonial thought-processes.

This means that for research our targets must be on problems that can provide the catalyst for thinking across boundaries as well as being of practical importance for the society in which we live. Provincial and federal funding bodies must therefore be discouraged from looking at research as being limited to one discipline and as providing an "answer" to the expediencies of short-term policy. A bold financing gesture on the lines of Chicago research of the 1920's and 1930's is likely to provide both the intellectual and the policy results in a way that piecemeal research does not. This goes beyond the dichotomy between 'applied' and 'pure' research. It is the recognition that an intellectual culture emerges out of the practical realities of a society, but that reality is not the segmentation of experience by artificial categories of either academic discipline or public policy.

But we cannot maintain the illusion that this will be done in the universities alone (if the various bureaucracies maintain their present course, it may not be possible to do it at all). The real problem is to work towards a social milieu where ideas are taken seriously. This can only be done in a context where to be an intellectual and *engagé* are synonymous. The context for this cannot be the university until it is radically transformed from being a knowledge factory and the willing mouthpiece of the dominant culture. To date the arenas for this intellectual development are few. The *Forum, Canadian Dimension,* some of the new publishing ventures, the marxisant sects, some forms of community action, are among the examples. But what we have is ambience, not movement, ideas but little creativity, radical politics but hardly any theory.

I do not mean, of course, that to create an intellectual culture is to graft professors on to a radical movement any more than that we must attempt to recreate an Augustan age with our Popes, Johnsons and Boswells making witty conversations in teashops or pubs. What I mean is close to what Max Weber implied in his analysis of the consequences of the dissolution of the monasteries in England. "For when asceticism was carried out of monastic cells into everyday life and began to dominate worldly morality, it did its part in building the tremendous cosmos of the modern economic order. . . . ." If we liberate academics from their cells, they must cease to treat 'knowledge' as sacred and a priestly calling, but the public arena in which the battles of everyday life are fought, in which the commonsense experience of daily reality is pitted against the hardened categorical thought of the professor. The experience will be as uncomfortable for our universities as for our politicians. But if they refuse to liberate themselves, the academics will find their cells becomng more cramped, their knowledge less relevant to daily reality, and all the decisions affecting their destinies made by those (such as the politician-lawyers) for whom ideas are only basic commodities in a market in which action is simply a replication of the status quo.

Ten Years to Know-where

Hugh A. Stevenson

During the past ten years there have been many exciting developments in Canadian education. Exactly a decade ago, for example, we had a vintage year: the Second Canadian Conference on Education in March 1962 marked the national dimension of our concerns; Quebec, in those innocent days of the Quiet Revolution was deeply immersed in the famous Parent Commission and the English edition of *The Impertinences of Brother Anonymous* introduced many Canadians to *joual* and the significance of language rather than religion to national identity for French-speaking citizens; both Marshall McLuhan and Northrop Frye produced extremely significant works for educators; Ontario gave birth to the ill-fated Robarts Plan and William Davis almost simultaneously; in British Columbia and New Brunswick royal commissions dealt with higher education; elsewhere teacher training, research and adult education received attention. Annually more and more money was being spent to revitalize public education from days of enforced neglect during the depression and war. The passivity of the 1950's disappeared; our concerns were now qualitative as well as quantitative. Canadians had faith in public education and were secure in their conviction that more education held forth rich rewards not only for individuals but also the nation too. We thought education was in a state of ferment but we faced the difficulties ahead in a gay party mood, with optimistic spirits, confident in our own ability to inaugurate a renaissance in

Canadian school systems. It was a memorable time for Canadian education, one with a delightful sense of urgency about it which left no margin for delay. Unfortunately, the margin for error was not reduced correspondingly.

After drinking lustily of the vintage grape, in 1972 we seem to have little more than a monumental hangover with only bitter dregs left for hair-of-the-dog treatments. Now, in the harsh light of the morning after the decade before, little remains of public education as we thought and felt about it in 1962. During ten years it appears that we gambled the intellectual and material resources of a generation on a spree that has left us Know-Where! We are left now with little more than the sober task of cleaning up the debris of our revelry, plagued, as we do it, by recriminations and soul-searching self-analysis. Any day we are likely to arrive at the self-righteous conclusion that, once again, original sin has foiled man's vain aspirations toward perfection in public education. Then we shall have found the ultimate justification for severe penance in new excesses of retrenchment and accountability pursued with inquisitorial vengeance.

During a decade in which we experienced more public educational change than in any other comparable period in our history, Canadians failed to achieve truly fundamental reforms. We became fascinated with enlarging the institution and giving its branches variety, yet we did little but talk about relating its complex functions to a rapidly changing society. Many changes were made with little or no thought of the chain reaction that had been initiated and the essentiality of integrating societal development and educational reform. Like fuddled business executives after too many liquid lunches, we over-advertised, over-produced and too often overlooked quality control. We precipitated a crash by failing to understand the worth of our own product and the complexity of marketing it. From boom to bust the pendulum has swung with disgusting regularity for anyone with a shred of faith left in the view that rational men have a large degree of control over their own destinies.

The greatest illusion of the Sixties was the mistaken belief that we made significant changes in Canadian public education. It has no substance. One can only take comfort in small achievements. Our real legacy from the period is the realization that we did not learn how to make fundamental changes which led to genuine reforms. Despite its obvious negative qualities, acceptance of that concept as our inheritance is extremely important.

Ten years' experience with scientific and technological developments has worsened our confusion concerning educational change and deepened the present crisis. Technology in education has proven to be a congenial enough bedmate, yet at the same time a wantonly fickle and terribly expensive mistress. Not surprisingly her relationship has not lived up to the glamour and mystery of first encounters. As with politicians, when the electorate eventually tires of promises concerning unrealized potential, among teachers there has been too much frustration and not enough fulfilment in the purported educational enrichment of technological applications in the classroom.

The relationship between educators and other academic disciplines looked more promising a decade ago than it had for a great many years. It had the makings of strong leadership in the reform of public education. But that too has proven to be a disillusioning experience leading to no fundamental changes. The fault rests with both sides. Too few Canadian social scientists, humanists and scientists wished to know education well enough to make a significant contribution; too few educators have persisted in whatever attempts they made to meet traditional disciplines. Some have come to terms with the problem by ignoring it completely. As a result interdisciplinary work has generally been unsuccessful if it was tried. Academic disciplines have not come to know and contribute to the one professional discipline which by its very nature touches all other branches of scholarly activity and the major interests of our society.

The Canadian literature on educational reform has been

singularly disappointing. It tended to be scattered, appeared infrequently and often dealt in extremes which, translated into solutions, quickly evaporated into intellectualizing. The imported reformist literature has been no better. Reim-Illichian alternatives have certainly made mouths water among Canadians starved of educational ideas. Yet close examination shows them to be little more than a rather lumpy mixture, the powdered eggs of intellectual foreign aid, too badly scrambled to sit well in shrunken Canadian stomachs. Other pre-cooked foreign products which we import rather faddishly from time to time are sometimes more palatable. However, they often need a great deal more cooking before being placed on Canadian tables and they suffer rather badly in the reheating. One should not underestimate the global dimensions to contemporary educational problems; certainly we should not ignore them. However, at the same time we cannot hope to approach realistic involvement in that level of activity while we are distracted from our own fundamental problems. Whether home grown or imported, the recent literature on educational reform has not filled the vacuum. It has not helped us to make practical progress in coming to grips with the central problem of how to reform Canadian education for large numbers of people.

While periodical literature gave Canadians a steady diet of complaint in the last ten years, both its outpourings and that of the isolated radical critics have not offered much in the way of how to change. In that vital area of public education we have clung tenaciously to Royal Commissions, ministers' committees and so on – all very traditional forms of public investigation with much the same result we have always had from them in Canada. They have generated a great deal of public discussion; they have even identified some very important formats. The fact remains that their implementation depends ultimately on political desirability, not educational need. Consequently, the record of change resulting directly from them has not been very impressive. Royal Commissions have become the burying ground for the ideas of some of our best thinkers.

These traditional measures have helped little in reforming public education quickly enough to meet the needs of people living in a rapidly changing society. Current estimates of the time needed to implement significant changes throughout an educational system still run between ten and forty years. By generating public discussion and identifying issues to be solved we have made public education a matter of consistent concern to Canadians. Yet in doing so without improving our success rate at implementing solutions we have done little more than decrease public faith in their systems of schooling. This effect has been heightened by the constant barrage of propaganda they experienced for most of that period which told them their faith would be rewarded materially if only they and their children drank deeper at the fount of learning. Of course this was a hollow promise as many people are now beginning to realize.

Similarly, we have made no real progress in the relationship between education, employability and the economics of abundance in a society with limited resources. Hard times now are harder for those with a heavy investment in their own education. When they fall, their expectations have farther to drop and are likely to land much harder. It is little wonder that one sees the disenchantment of youth shift from the dissatisfaction with institutions of a few years ago to a tendency to abandon those institutions and criticize the society that allowed them to perpetrate the myth that education enabled one to make a productive contribution to one's society and to be rewarded accordingly. That more have not opted out may be a transitory phenomenon indicative of their basic conservatism. They continue to attend schools because the immediate alternatives are not very attractive and a diploma or a degree can be seen as an insurance policy which will pay off in better times. Such thinking is very characteristic of Canadian society – but it will be a threadbare argument if bad times persist. Its appeal is based entirely on faith in the cyclical, accidental return of better days – the economic counterpart to the pendulum theory of educational change.

Politicians may react to the crisis in public education by trying cynically to exploit the disillusionment of the electorate and making the schools a scapegoat. They have the means through control of the legislative process and there is some evidence to suggest that such a choice has already been made. Budget cuts and regulations originate in provincial capitals and are explained politically as responsible necessities. Bad planning is seldom examined in public and the mechanism of cutting expenditures is passed to the local level where criticism is likely to be most severe. The shambles that is made of quality in teaching and learning is buried in the experience between students and teachers. Puzzled by complexities and confusion in public education, their faith already shaken, often parents realize too late the consequences such activities have on the lives of their children.

But there is an obstacle now to this time-honoured method of retrenchment. Not only is the public more astute but so too are teachers. Given their numbers and the power teachers can exert collectively through their professional organizations, they constitute a real threat to provincial educational moguls. That threat and the political reaction is now very apparent to the newspaper-reading public who are told of teachers' insisting on the right to strike in Quebec even though the legislature has rescinded its original grant to do so. In British Columbia the petty foolishness of the Bennett government, displayed recently in attempting to curtail the power of professional teachers by rescinding the legislation making payment of fees to the B.C.T.F. mandatory and automatic, has infuriated the Federation's members. Their reaction was entirely predictable and swift. They fought the government, increased their loyalty to their professional organizations and, at time of writing, were attempting to deduct a day's pay from each teacher for a political war chest to oust the Social Credit government. This move was greeted with an injunction but the lesson to be learned from the situation is clear. Just as the public is more reluctant to accept traditional political rhetoric in place of solutions, so too are teachers.

In the midst of all this upheaval, disillusionment and conflict the power of educational authority remains centralized, sedentary and safe, thoroughly entrenched in *provincial* control. And this is precisely what is at the root of our present difficulties. Our archaic, historical conception of educational democratization and the smoke screen of equalizing opportunity allows provincial governments to continue exercising their power in a futile effort to meet problems which can only be solved by concerted *federal* action. Such ineffective devices as the Council of Provincial Ministers of Education are symptomatic of last-ditch attempts to keep educational decision-making power in provincial political hands. Its most useful function would be to take the initiative in devising a rational framework for Canadian education which would allow provincial ministers to abdicate their powers gracefully and without loss of face.

During the last decade we flirted fitfully with greater federal involvement in education but restricted the relationship to pay-offs on a short-term basis with no fundamental alteration in the prospects for improved education. Most important, we ignored the fundamental relationship between education, use of human resources and societal development and satisfied ourselves with training and retraining more technicians on an ad hoc basis without sufficient attention to their employment prospects. The only solution is to identify the relationship between education and the economy and devise relevant programs, which is impossible with our disunited and fragmented provincial systems.

Provincial organization may have served us well enough in a 19th century society. However, those conditions have gone forever and it is time we adjusted the educational mechanism, its organization, and the power bases within the structure to meet present circumstances. While we have devised local systems which are in many respects educationally self-sufficient, we have not altered the narrow provincial control of their functions and recognized the truly national dimensions of most Canadian educational problems. Education must be depoliticized on the provincial level and at the same time kept responsible to the public who finance it.

The solution does not lie in replacing provincial control with a federal bureaucracy of unparallelled size, complexity and remoteness. It lies in a readjustment of power in new institutional frameworks which remove control of education from provincial political hands and give recognition to national needs. We need new, delicately balanced, federal and local educational structures which will foster a new form of trusteeship, one which preserves democratic political responsibility in protecting societal interests, yet allows teachers the freedom to behave with full professional responsibility in serving those interests.

It is an intriguing question to consider what might happen if suddenly all Ministries of Education were padlocked. Except for funding and the legalistic business of certification of teachers and graduates, public education would not suffer greatly. Local jurisdictions working closely with post-secondary institutions can now reform curriculum, teach pupils and perform all necessary educational services. Once funding and the legal responsibility for some basic aspects of education were transferred to a new national agency, the reasons for retaining provincial control of education would evaporate.

The arguments for federal direction of education combined with local control are stronger now than they have ever been in the past. Only at the national level can we come to grips with the relationship between the economy and education. Then we might finally devise an equitable tax structure for education that reduces, if not replaces, our clinging to a property-based system. Finally, we might achieve real equality of educational opportunity by confronting squarely the question of regional disparities.

Of course, the main stumbling block to all this is the

jealously guarded prerogatives of provincial governments enshrined in the B.N.A. Act defining education as a provincial responsibility. Constitutional reform is not merely essential for the national identity crisis which the sixties generated, as well as the ever-present menace of Amercanization, it is also crucial to realistic educational reform. Provincial autonomy is a weak argument when it cannot solve problems. It may be difficult to reform our constitutional arrangements but it may also be vital to national interest to do so. We are familiar with economic and political arguments to this end. That education may also join in the chorus for constitutional reform may come as something of a surprise. But is there any real alternative except such a radical response to the rising tide of public and professional opinion expressing dissatisfaction with education?

The most obvious argument against a new national structure and revised balance of power between federal, local and professional involvement is, of course, the view that Quebec would never be content to join in such a national system of education. Her particular interests, as a province unlike the others, could not be satisfied. While this may be the most serious deterrent to the success of a national system, it may also be a risk that Canadians have to take in an effort to improve Canadian education. If fundamental educational improvement can only be achieved by a united approach with national leadership and a high degree of local autonomy and diversity in the practical details of education, then Quebec's possible objections become unreasonable. Diversity and variety in local jurisdictions, large enough to be managed efficiently and not too small to entrench parochialism, provide the solution. Meeting national objectives, priorities and standards does not mean the abolition of local identity and an oppressive sameness in education throughout the land. It simply means removing provincial control in practice and in law by removing an unnecessary political middleman in the education industry. Educators would be freer than ever to teach and meet the needs of a local community within the framework of Canadian priorities and objectives essential for the welfare of all. Critical public discussion would remain central in such a nationally reorganized system and would assure more vitality than our present mechanisms. Democratic rights which are fundamental to our political, social and economic philosophy would be protected in a large degree of localized autonomy. Such a reorganization would allow us to make fundamental reforms in education.

Ten years ago we had three things that are worth reviving now – a firm faith in the value of public education, belief that we could achieve fundamental reforms to meet rapidly changing circumstances, and a national dimension to our concerns. Why not now? A national system, de-politicized on the provincial level but carefully coordinated with national goals, largely left to the responsible trusteeship of educators with sufficient latitude for local initiative to generate variety in the process and stimulate public involvement, is worth attempting. It may be not only our sole viable alternative to the present crisis but also an extremely positive approach with genuine benefits for the survival of a strong Canadian identity. The need to find out is more crucial now than it has ever been. We have just experienced ten years to find that we have arrived Know-Where in terms of fundamental education reforms. With luck and concerted national effort we may have ten years to alter the present drift and demoralization sufficiently to revitalize public education and avoid the disastrous consequences of failure to do so. We are in a position to solve our educational problems if we have the courage to make basic reforms.

Who Killed the Goose?

Howard Fluxgold

Education, the golden-haired child of the Fifties and Sixties has become the whipping boy of the Seventies. During the Fifties and Sixties our favourite disc jockeys exhorted us to "stay in school, don't be a fool." Even our favourite rock'n roll stars were telling us that the way to wealth and happiness was through education. But by painful experience we have learned that more education does not cure all our ills. Many have become disillusioned (and unemployed) with the educational segment of our society which has failed to live up to its promises – ill-considered though they may have been.

The result is that many are questioning the value of spending increased amounts of money or time on education; an education which has utterly failed the poor, has not brought the promised rewards to the middle classes, and has increasingly irritated the wealthy.

During the Fifties the public's hopes for prosperity were raised by a relatively small group of prestigious, and doubtless well-intentioned medicine men who deliberately encouraged the public to believe that the universities were an economic and cultural wonder drug or cure-all. Immediately after World War II the Veteran's Rehabilitation program sent thousands to universities across Canada. Enrolments increased abruptly and universities were forced to provide for a rapidly expanding student population with little advance warning. Universities handled the job admirably, producing graduates who readily found employment in a rapidly expanding post-war economy. But just as abruptly as enrolments had increased, they began to fall off in the late 1940's as the veterans graduated and no one took their place. University personnel had had their collective appetites whetted by the well-earned prestige, popularity and increased financial support associated with the veterans' program. They had no desire to return to pre-war conditions and saw that with decreasing enrolments, staff hired to teach the veterans would have to be dismissed. At this point the National Conference of Canadian Universities (NCCU), the association of Canadian universities swung into action.

It is perhaps unseemly to speak of the universities as a pressure group or lobby, in the same class as the Canadian Manufacturers Association. Nevertheless, the NCCU managed to persuade the Royal Commission on National Development in the Arts, Letters and Sciences (the Massey Commission) to recommend that the federal government financially support universities. It also successfully convinced Prime Minister Louis St. Laurent that his government ought to establish for the first time a system of per capita grants to universities. In 1950, a year before the Commission reported, St. Laurent told the NCCU that its request for aid would have a better chance for success if it were able to gain wide public support.[2] Taking the hint, the NCCU hired the John Price Jones public relations firm to help organize a public speaking campaign by university presidents. The campaign was designed to coincide with the release of the Commission's report which the NCCU had reason to believe would support the idea of federal financial aid to universities. The NCCU issued the following instructions to its members who were going out to rally public support:

(a) *That it was essential that the Canadian universities should unanimously support the recommendations of the Massey Commission* Report *when it was published. . . The* Report, *would . . . probably recommend* that the government should help the universities in some substantial way, and criticism would not get any alternative plan adopted.

(b) That there should be no mention of the Massey Commission Report in any features or other publicity before the Report was actually tabled in the House.

(c) That all speakers or writers using statistics should be careful that these did not conflict with those of the John Price Jones Manual. This would avoid harmful arguments.

(d) That any member of the Committee who had interesting facts concerning payment of staff, fees, scholarships, etc., should send them as quickly as possible to the Secretary for use in the John Price Jones Manual.

(e) That the campaign should start on the 1st April (1951).

(f) That at every forum of publicity the contribution universities were making to national defence should be stressed.

(g) That there should not be any attempt to persuade the general public to send a flood of letters to members of parliament, but that those in a position to do so should make personal references to secure the interest of members of the Cabinet and of the House. . .[3]

The search for truth takes winding roads. The initial publicity campaign, and there were to be others, was designed primarily to gain public support for a course of action that the government had already decided to follow. The university presidents had been successful in exerting influence on the Massey Commission and the federal government. Their public pronouncements however, sowed the seeds of their current difficulties.

The initial campaign concentrated on the need for equal opportunity for all. In 1950 President G. Edward Hall of the University of Western Ontario told the Ridley College Old Boys Association:

Fees went up so high in five years that many bright pupils in high schools can't go on to university because their parents haven't the money. I don't think I'm being socialist minded when I say that higher education must be available for all those capable of absorbing it. . .4

A year later, President G. P. Gilmour of McMaster University announced, somewhat prematurely, that "the day when universities could be the darling philanthropy of wealthy individuals and their special privilege has ended. . ."5

The public did not respond unfavourably to such idealistic goals. On June 19, 1951, St. Laurent was able to announce safely that his government would support universities at the rate of 50c per capita to a total of approximately $7,100,000. St. Laurent warned that this was not a permanent university grant scheme and that the aid was designed "to maintain quality rather than to increase existing facilities."6 St. Laurent obviously believed that the federal government could become half pregnant. Although funds had to be voted yearly through the Appropriations Act, per capita grants to universities were awarded annually and increased frequently between 1951 and 1966.

Each increase was preceded by an effective buildup of public sentiment by the education interests by raising hopes for wealth, happiness and continued prosperity. At the same time there were warnings of economic and social consequences if more money were not allocated to education. Education and motherhood went hand in hand.

For example, in 1953, the NCCU decided to begin "a broad program to bring to the attention of the Canadian public the vital need for increased financial aid to the universities. . ."7 A publicity committee was established under Claude Bissell then (1954) Vice-President of the University of Toronto. The Committee decided that:

There was to be a trans-Canada speaking tour in which various university officials and faculty members would participate. This major activity would be supported by radio programs, newspaper and magazine articles, and above all, by special local arrangements . . . The general topic for the speakers was "The Crisis of the Universities". . .8

Emphasis was placed on the financial difficulties of the universities, the need for the public to support the universities as well as the need to provide places for ever-increasing enrolments. The major emphasis, however, was placed on the value of education to the economy. Typical of the argument was the declaration of Dr. G. Edward Hall. In a speech to the Board of Trade Club of Toronto in 1956 he claimed that "the university graduate is indispensable to Canadian economic, technological and scientific development."9

Perhaps the single most important factor in convincing St. Laurent to double the per capita grants to $1.00 in 1956-57 was a preliminary report of the Royal Commission on Canada's Economic Prospects (Gordon Commission). The Commissioners felt it "our bounden duty to call attention . . . to the vital part which the universities must play in our expanding and increasing complex economy. . ."10 They recommended that "a deliberate and sustained effort be made to raise the quality and standards of Canadian universities to among the highest prevailing anywhere in the world. . ."11 This was in response to the NCCU brief which warned:

There has been a serious deterioration in the relative economic position of university staff which is affecting not merely the ability to recruit and hold staff but more ominously the interest of the ablest students in academic careers. . .12

The Commissioners suggested that teachers' salary scales be raised "substantially". This would raise "the whole status of the teaching profession in Canada." As a result, it would become "increasingly easier to persuade young Canadians of high quality to enter the teaching profession." This prediction has come true although the results are a mixed blessing.

On January 29, 1957 St. Laurent told the House of Commons that per capita grants would be doubled to $1.00. He said, in part:

> *. . . no government which bears any share of responsibility for the future economic development of this country can allow a solution to pressing financial problems of the universities to go by default.*13

The universities' campaign for greater support received an unexpected boost when the Russians launched the first Sputnik that year. Amid the general handwringing over the deficiencies of Canadian education in comparison to Russia, the universities injected a patriotic note into their continuing campaign for more and better education. Shortly after the grants were raised to $1.50 for 1958/59, Murray Ross, Vice-President of the University of Toronto told the Canadian Club of Toronto that, "the survival of Western democracy could depend on accelerated public support for universities."14 At the same time the Toronto *Globe and Mail* reported that:

> *Canada's advertising industry has prepared a million-dollar coast-to-coast advertising campaign to inform Canadians of the problems of education . . . the campaign will be donated as a public service by the advertising industry and publishing and broadcasting media.*15

While the disc jockeys told us to "stay in school," Claude Bissell, now President of the University of Toronto told the Board of Trade Club: "Universities may well become the rallying points of our society . . . strong universities are essential for prosperity – prosperity that keeps a balance between things and ideas, prosperity that unites power with peace."16

Grants were increased again in 1962/63 to $2.00 and in 1966/67 to $5.00, the latter in accordance with the recommendation of the report of the Commission on the Financing of Higher Education in Canada (the Bladen Commission). This Commission was sponsored by the Association of Universities and Colleges of Canada (AUCC) a successor to the NCCU. The $5.00 per capita grant was in effect for one year, 1966/67. In 1966 Prime Minister Pearson announced the government's withdrawal from direct financial support of universities in favour of a tax transfer agreement with the provinces.

For fifteen years from 1950 to 1965 Canadians were bombarded by admen who told of the benefits of a university education. At the root of the campaign was the claim that more education would lead to a rapidly expanding economy and greater wealth for all – but especially for those with a degree. J. Bascom St. John, the education columnist for the *Globe and Mail*, writing in the late 1950's said:

> . . . *one of the prime causes of the surge of demand to get into university is simply a sort of avarice. Our young people read that a university degree adds about $100,000 to the lifetime earnings of a graduate. . . Almost unavoidably our universities have been catering to this demand.*17

Nevertheless, by the late Fifties some provincial governments and the federal government were beginning to realize that universities were not the only method of supplying trained manpower. There was a shortage of skilled labour at this time. The Department of Labour attributed the problem to the fact that "Canada has never trained enough persons to meet the demand for skilled workers. In recent years European sources of skilled workers are drying up as most European countries are short of labour."18

The solution to the problem produced by the Diefenbaker government was the Technical and Vocational Training Assistance Act, 1961/66. Among other things, this Act provided a considerable portion of the funds required to construct the community colleges. It also provided funds for support

for high school courses in which at least one-half of the school time is devoted to technical, commercial or other vocational subjects. The courses must be designed to prepare students for entry into employment or for further vocational or technical training.[19]

Serious questions were raised, however, as to the effectiveness of the Diefenbaker program. The provinces selected the courses and many had no relation to the skills needed in the economy. A large proportion of the funds were being used to train young students below the school leaving age rather than older persons who needed a skill to obtain a job. The program was missing many in the lowest income groups. At the same time it benefited areas of high employment, while neglecting areas of greatest unemployment.

In 1966, Prime Minister Pearson announced that the TVTA Act would be replaced by a new Manpower program. In order to gain greater control of manpower retraining, the federal government decided to support students to retrain for specific jobs required in the economy. In other words, the province would provide the courses and the federal government would decide whether or not it would purchase them. While acknowledging that education was a provincial prerogative, Pearson stated that the federal government ought to provide "a basic 'economic equality' for the provinces, together with equality of educational and employment opportunity for all Canadians."[20] Amplifying on this theme of equality of opportunity, Jean Marchand told the House of Commons:

This new program is an integral part of a national manpower policy whose basic purpose is to bring economic opportunity within the reach of Canadian workers. . . We want to provide a second chance to the people who need it most. These are the men and women who missed the chance to acquire a skill during their youth or whose skill has been made obsolete by technological change.[21]

The Manpower Program to date has failed to achieve its objectives, if the unemployment figures are taken as a measure of economic opportunity as well as equality of economic opportunity among the provinces. In 1966, the year Pearson announced the new program, 3.6 per cent of the labour force was unemployed. In 1971 the rate was 6.4 per cent, representing a sharp decrease in economic opportunity. In 1966 the unemployment rate in the Atlantic Region was 6.4 per cent; five years later it had risen to 8.6 per cent. Moreover, the difference between the unemployment rate in the Atlantic Region, the region with the highest unemployment rate, and the Prairie Region, the region with the lowest rate, decreased by only 0.2 per cent in five years. This indicates that there has been practically no equalizing of economic opportunity across Canada over the last five years. As far as providing "a second chance to the people who need it most" the Manpower program has utterly failed.

Poverty in Canada, the forgotten Report of the Special Senate Committee on poverty said:

As presently operated, the Canada Manpower Program will inevitably have a limited effect on poverty. . . Manpower programs aimed at improving and up-dating the skills of the labour force are too narrow and limited not only in terms of anti-poverty objectives but in terms of meaningful development of the human resources of the nation.[22]

This is not the first time, unfortunately, that promises made to the public have gone unfulfilled. The universities proclaimed that a university education should be available to all those with ability not just those with enough money to pay for it. Yet after an expenditure of over $400 million on per capita grants and over $1 million on the TVTA program, the position of the poor has not significantly improved. *The Real Poverty Report* said that "Education . . . has failed as a weapon against the transmission of poverty from one generation to another. . ."23 It reported that while "the children of the poor . . . are tending to stay in school one or two years longer than their parents . . . so are the children of the rich. The gap between the two groups is not closing."24 The report criticized the federal government for limiting its financial support for education to universities, "a place the children of the poor usually don't get to." Although the universities claimed that education must be available for all, their efforts to make this claim a reality have been a dismal failure. The Report concludes: "The various improvements in the educational system that came about with the increased demand of the 1950's and 60's has not . . . done much good for the children of the poor."25

We have been told by the universities that the university graduate is indispensable to economic, technological and scientific development. Even the Economic Council of Canada (ECC) agreed in 1964, that:

*During the post war period it has become increasingly apparent that the future prosperity of a nation will depend in large measures on its success in creating and maintaining an adequate supply of professional, technical, managerial and other highly skilled manpower.*26

But the recent university or college graduate has been unable to perceive the "apparent" need for highly trained or skilled manpower. Indeed, he is increasingly likely to be unemployed. The Technical Service Council, a non-profit placement service sponsored by 390 Canadian employers reported that industry employs only 19 per cent of Canada's Ph.D.'s in engineering and science. Only 14 per cent of engineers and scientists in Canada are employed in research and development.27 According to these figures, one might conclude that Canada's technological and scientific development is at a virtual standstill and its prosperity in extreme jeopardy. That's not what the universities promised.

The universities cried out for more money for teachers' salaries so that more and better people would be attracted to the profession.Yet, when this campaign for more teachers was starting to pay off in an increased supply of ph.d.'s, universities continued to seek teaching staff outside the country. Worse still some are now firing professors owing to a lack of students and grants. With brilliant hindsight the ECC now suggests that "with the growing abundance of highly educated people in our work force, post-secondary education must not be sold to students and the public as an unfailing means to a good job and a comfortable income."28 This seems to be the new theme that the education interests are playing. Dr. Frank Kelly of the Science Council of Canada puts it in a suitably understated way: "I think we have been a little hasty in expecting financial rewards (from education). . . In one sense, this has not materialized." And he adds, "Education is not about jobs."29 Indeed not. The unemployment statistics tell the story. In 1953, shortly after the beginning of massive aid to education, 3 per cent of the work force was unemployed. Almost twenty years later, after millions of dollars have been spent on education, the unemployment rate has more than doubled to 6.4 per cent in 1971. The unemployment rate for those between 14 and 24 years of age has almost tripled from 4.5 per cent in 1953 to 11.4 per cent in 1971.

There seems therefore, to be a large divergence between the promises and the reality. Is it any wonder, then, that the public in this country has become frustrated and disillusioned with education? Students are showing their discontent by withdrawing. The drop-out rate in Metro Toronto high schools for 1971/72 was 22 per cent higher than the previous year. As one official explained, "There were a lot of payoffs mouthed for school, but there's not a single one the kid is sure of getting now. Jobs, integrity because of the academic sequence – none of that is sure now."30

Fewer of those who graduate from high school are going to university. "I'm sick of school and I'm not prepared to put in another three years for a B.A. that isn't worth anything," said one high schol student close to graduation.31 Meanwhile, the papers blare their bold headlines: HUNDREDS OF GRADUATES WON'T FIND JOBS, or, BLEAK AND DISMAL JOB PROSPECTS FACE U OF T GRADUATES. Education, in the eyes of the public, is no longer a "motherhood" issue, but merely a drain on the economy. Governments have responded by reducing financial support to all levels of education. Those who made such totally unrealistic promises must bear a major portion of the responsibility for destroying the golden goose.

The goose may be dead but we cannot ignore the growing dissatisfaction and frustration with the educational system. The public has become increasingly aware that education does not necessarily lead to national or individual prosperity, despite the vast sums of public money spent on it. The public is becoming increasingly more frustrated with its inability to affect the direction of education and is less willing to pay the considerable expense for education which produces few tangible results. As a result, governments have found it politically feasible to reduce drastically expenditure on education.

The problem, basically, revolves around the inability or unwillingness to define the goals of education realistically. We know now that education won't by itself save democracy, nor will it guarantee or create good jobs with high pay. It may complement or support viable economic and social policy but it is not a substitute for it.

The first step towards defining such goals must be to permit the people whose children are being educated to have a more direct influence in designing these goals. The massive bureaucracy which now administers our educational systems effectively thwarts any public attempt to become more involved in the direction of education. The decision-making process has become too distant for the public to have any real influence on it. The growing trend towards centralization is gradually strangling the interested individual in a mass of red tape. It is making change more difficult and, as many students claim, education less relevant to living today. The trend toward centralization, in the name of economic efficiency must be stopped. Local committees must be given the opportunity to make the important decision as to what kind of education they want in their schools and universities. This would change the direction of the decision-making process. No longer would the central government "consult" the people concerned before making its decision. (Many now believe the central government has its mind made up prior to consultation.) Local authorities could use the wealth of human resources and expertise amassed by the central government on a consultative basis in formulating programs. If the people at the local level who actually pay the bill for education make poor decisions, they themselves must accept the consequences of *their* decisions.

It may be that under such a system of local control, some communities may require unequal treatment. Economically depressed urban and rural areas, for example, must be given the additional funds necessary to deal with such an abominable situations as described in the report *Poverty in Canada*: "20 per cent of the adult population of the northern prairies are functionally illiterate – that is, have less than four years of schooling."[32] *The Real Poverty Report* was also highly critical of education in Canada:

> *Poor children . . . are not receiving a fair share of public investment in education. And even the share they do get tends to do them little good. Education in Canada is designed by and for the members of the middle class; it is aimed quite specifically at the average. . .*[33]

It is unfortunate that the federal government has not seen any need to encourage the provinces to seek remedies for such problems. Its financial support is limited to adult and post-secondary education. Increased financial support for educating the poor might just lead to decreasing welfare payments, a very tangible result.

We are now at a crucial stage of public education in Canada. Society is seriously questioning the usefulness of an expensive public educational system. It has discovered the hollowness of the old platitudes. If a dynamic public education system is to be developed its purposes and functions must be explained to the public honestly and involve the public directly.

FOOTNOTES

1. Much of the research into the role of the NCCU in the establishment of per capita grants was conducted by Professor David A. A. Stager of the University of Toronto, and can be found in *"Federal Government Grants to Canadian Universities, 1951-1966,"* Institute For Policy Analysis, University of Toronto, Working Paper No. 7205.
2. *Proceeding of the National Conference of Canadian Universities,* 1951, p. 46.
3. *Minutes of the Executive Committee,* National Conference of Canadian Universities, March 17, 1951.
4. *Globe and Mail,* February 25, 1950.
5. *Ibid.,* May 26, 1951.
6. House of Commons, *Debates,* 1951, Vol. V., p. 4278.
7. "Report of the Finance Committee" in National Conference of Canadian Universities, *Proceedings,* 1954, p. 79.
8. "Report of the Publicity Committee," in National Conference of Canadian Universities, *Proceedings,* 1955, p. 90.
9. *Globe and Mail,* February 7, 1956.
10. *Royal Commission on Canada's Economic Prospects, Preliminary Report,* Ottawa, 1956, p. 752.
11. *Ibid.,* p. 753.
12. NCCU, "Submission of Canadian Universities to the Royal Commission on Canada's Economic Prospects," (mimeographed), March 6, 1956, p. 18.
13. House of Commons, *Debates,* Vol. 1, January 29, 1957, p. 752.
14. *Globe and Mail,* December 1, 1958.
15. *Ibid.*
16. *Ibid.,* March 3, 1959.
17. *Ibid.,* June 23, 1959.
18. Department of Labour, *Technical and Vocational Education in Canada,* Vol. 1, No. 1, summer 1962, p. 5.
19. Department of Labour, Technical and Vocational Training, *Annual Report,* 1964/65, p. 2.
20. *Federal Provincial Conference, Ottawa, October 24-28, 1966,* Ottawa, 1968, p. 18.

21. House of Commons, *Debates*, Vol. 13, March 3, 1967, p. 13737.
22. A Report of the Special Senate Committee, *Poverty in Canada*, Ottawa, 1971, p. 152.
23. I. Adams, W. Cameron, B. Hill, P. Penz, *The Real Poverty Report*, Edmonton, 1971, p. 217.
24. *Ibid.*, p. 218.
25. *Ibid.*, p. 225.
26. Economic Council of Canada, *First Annual Review, Economic Goals for Canada to 1970*, Ottawa, 1964, p. 160.
27. *Globe and Mail*, April 6, 1971.
28. Economic Council of Canada, *Eighth Annual Review, September, 1971*, Ottawa, 1971, p. 223.
29. *Globe and Mail*, April 6, 1971.
30. *Ibid.*, May 20, 1972.
31. *Toronto Star*, March 17, 1972.
32. The Report of the Special Senate Committee, *op.cit.*, p. 115.
33. Adams, Cameron, Hill and Penz, *op.cit.*, p. 221.

Where Have All the Free Schools Gone?

A conversation with the editors of *This Magazine is About Schools,* Bob Davis , Satu Repo and George Martell.

edited by Douglas Myers

Introduction

Since it began publishing in 1966, *This Magazine is About Schools* has consistently produced some of the most lively, stimulating educational writing in North America. Its stance was anti-establishment; its tone direct and personal. Although it was never committed to a narrow dogmatic position, over the past year or two the emphasis in *This Magazine* has been shifting markedly.

In the context of this collection of articles on education the *Canadian Forum* thought it especially important to talk to three people who have been centrally involved with *This Magazine* since its inception. Besides his work on the magazine, Bob Davis was one of the founders of The Everdale Place, a well known free school on a farm outside Toronto. Similarly, Satu Repo and George Martell were part of a downtown Toronto free school called Point Blank. Davis is no longer at Everdale and has given up his editorship of *This Magazine;* presently he is working with the daycare centre movement on the University of Toronto campus and teaching at the Ontario Institute for Studies in Education. Point Blank school is no longer in existence. Satu Repo, however, now works full time as managing editor of *This Magazine;* George Martell remains co-editor, is working on a book, and is teaching at Atkinson College, York University.

Clearly, for all three, this is a period of reassessment and transition. We think that what they have to say about their experience over the past six years, and the conclusions they have drawn from it, will be of great interest to those seriously interested in educational and social reform.

* * *

MYERS: *Reading the things you three have written over the past several years, it seems to me that if there has been a central theme in* This Magazine, *it has been the search for an effective means of fundamental educational and social change. Some of what seem at first like complete contradictions or reversals of direction are the result of deciding that this or that approach isn't working and something else ought to be tried. And there seems to have been a continuing debate about what was and was not working from the very beginning – there has never been much collective certainty in the tone of* This Magazine.

REPO: It has always expressed various themes around a certain end of the spectrum – they have not been very far apart but they haven't been identical. I think that's what made the magazine interesting for us. The editors still have slightly different emphases, slightly different points of view, and we had to struggle with each other.

MYERS: *I was also struck by the fact that, although its tone is certainly not cool or detached, it has generally avoided sounding shrill in a sectarian kind of way – in fact it has had a rather tolerant tone.*

REPO: I think that has to do with the fact that the magazine was never part of a larger political group. It's a virtue some- times, but it also shows how individualistic we were. We were a group of friends who thought rather similarly about things, and we had known each other a long time, and so we started a magazine.

DAVIS: Yeah, some of the tolerance was the result of not being specifically political activists but being interested in political activism and writing about it. Much of what we were actually *doing* was the counter-culture, developing experimental education, free schools of various kinds. One of the changes in the magazine is that we're no longer concerned with just reporting left activist activity, particularly in the student group, without stopping to analyze what is at the root of it.

REPO: Before we were just digging it, no matter what was at the bottom of it.

MYERS: *Well, whatever the ingredients, the recipe seemed to work, because the magazine has an astonishingly high reputation. Who, in fact, does read it and how are they distributed – is it better known in California than in Ontario?*

DAVIS: Probably administrators who felt themselves to be somewhat liberal would read it, plus a lot of educated counter-culture people, liberal teachers. . .

REPO: And liberal parents. . .

MARTELL: But by far and away our largest group are teachers and education professionals, maybe 60 to 70 per cent. And our most recent count, I think, shows that a little more than half our readers are in the States.

MYERS: *That, of course raises the whole nationalist/continentalist issue, but before we get into that, can we talk a bit about how you got into working in and writing about education and schools and why you saw education as being especially relevant to social change generally? You all seem to have been really very successful at school and yet, afterwards, to have felt that there was something essential missing in your experience and that schools were dehumanizing places.*

REPO: It had to do with our current jobs as teachers and social workers, I guess. Beginning to reflect on the influence of education and other socializing institutions. Being a social worker brought me back to the details of the situation now – it wasn't just thinking of the past. It was sort of looking at these institutions and seeing what they were doing to people right now, and what we were doing in these institutions.

MYERS: *But not in the sense that this had crunched you personally.*

REPO: That's right. Although there was also the understanding how they had deformed us, not in very obvious ways. You know, the way bad success spoils people just as well as bad failure.

DAVIS: George and I both went to Dalhousie and I think that both of us assumed that we didn't feel called upon to analyze the university in a basic way while we were there. It wasn't seen as part of our function as students. It was partly one of the functions of the Fifties that made poets and intellectuals stress individual personal lives outside institutions as the most important thing.

REPO: People took the society for granted much more – taking for granted that one fitted in or, if one didn't, one had a problem. It was before a large number of people turned things around. The beats represented a pretty individual solution for a few.

MYERS: *But wasn't the counter-culture movement in the 1960's also very concerned with personal lives?*

DAVIS: Well, my interest in the counter-culture was partly very different from the Fifties' stress on the personal, because it definitely proceeded from analyzing society as a whole. I participated in the C.U.C.N.D. and in S.U.P.A., and I saw connections between what I thought about schools and those things. I can say now that I wasn't primarily a political being the way I approached it, but it was nonetheless a general analytical reaction to the whole society. It was one of the things that thrust me in that direction. The other thing that made it different from the Fifties' stress on the personal was that I've always been interested in the tribal aspect of the counter-culture that got lots of people together, and not in people going off alone or with a few friends, like the Kerouac books, or attaching yourself to a guru in Japan. For me the commune was very important – the communal school. . .

REPO: For me it was the co-op.

DAVIS: Co-op houses, right.

REPO: We were all in co-op houses in the city, you know, before we got into this. And then there was the experience at Warrendale, the collective experience with kids and adults, which had a large influence on us, even those of us who didn't work there. These things had an important intellectual influence on us even before the counter-culture existed. It was sort of pre-counter culture – a Freudian kind of orientation. We would also look toward the group as the important thing, not so much the individual or psychiatrist-patient relationship. We were interested, too, in the therapeutic elements in family-size groups which we experienced in the co-ops and knew about in places like Warrendale, where they did amazing things with disturbed children in a family setting. That was an important inspiration for Everdale. A number of the people who were involved in starting it knew about Warrendale and were very impressed by it.

DAVIS: Some of the connections for Everdale are quite definite – on the theoretical level. Neill's Summerhill was the most important model for us. Neill spent a lot of time with Wilhelm Reich, and was analyzed by him and Reich took the parts of Freud that Satu was referring to and added his own sense of the communal.

MYERS: *I'm interested that Bob says what he did* proceeded from *an analysis of society, because it rather struck me in reading* This Magazine *that the basic motivation was the search for a more personally satisfying way of living – though in a group context – and that the experiences and frustrations of that process* led to *a more comprehensive social analysis.*

REPO: Well, I think, I would say for my part – the magazine started before counter-culture, before the student rebellions and all that. I started out with an intuitive reaction against the repressiveness of institutions like the school system and the school agencies, really looking at the kind of metaphysical, life and death forces in society and seeing those institutions as the death forces, and being sort of anarchistic and utopian in the kind of solutions I was thinking of. I saw the small communities as models that then might have influence on larger groups through being publicized in places like *This Magazine*. I thought of social change as much more a kind of poetic thing than a political thing. That's where I felt I was.

DAVIS: I think it's unfair to make this kind of dichotomy. Looking back now probably we might say that we were more practical people than analytical at that time, but it's not that we didn't have various analyses. We might now call them superficial, but we definitely had positions about society as a whole. It was based on a lot of faith that turned out not to be justified. It seemed to me to be supported by what was happening in 1968. All those university struggles seemed so exciting and so influential and it seemed that all these issues were very much related – especially in the French experience – to the whole working-class fight too.

REPO: Although we never made much of that – all our emphasis was on the students.

DAVIS: I'm trying to think in the back of my mind what must have convinced me that it was so central. I probably thought that it was going to happen like that eventually here too.

REPO: Well, we did think that the students were somehow in the vanguard of social change – for all kinds of reasons we were not so clear on. We took some things from McLuhan and some things from Marcuse and we had a sort of hodge-podge of reasons for believing that students had perhaps a strategic rôle in being a part of the work force formed around the technology. Bob had a much more serious critique of the family than either George or I had. I mean, he believed much more that the family had disintegrated and had not much meaning as a social unit and that, therefore, there had to be other institutions in the society.

MYERS: *Bob's writing has always had the greatest sense of urgency, of the three of you – the feeling of an impending cataclysm and, at the same time, tremendous optimism. It has almost a religious fervour – does this come out of your particular family background?*

DAVIS: Oh yeah, sure. I think the change has come in starting to accept the class analysis more and more. I realize now that behind this incredible faith I had in the counter-culture or in school upheavals there was the mistaken idea that society was more open than it is, that power was not as entrenched as it is, and the position of youth was very much removed from any control by the central parts of the society like the production system or the communications system. I think that was a very important weakness. For example, I was the one on the magazine's editorial board that was most excited by McLuhan's writings – and I still think there are aspects of communication which he analyzed in very interesting new ways. But the extent to which he announces that society has already changed in a total way – I now think that's not just wrong – it's vicious in fact, because it involves telling, say, the Vietnamese that nationalism is out of date. . . . So, to understand how this society works and, hopefully, how to change it, requires a lot of very serious analysis and thought and it requires analyzing aspects of society *not* having directly to do with schools.

MYERS: *In 1969, if I recall correctly, you printed a very harsh critique of* This Magazine's *position by Satu's sister, Marjaleena Repo, in which she accused you all, but especially George, of indulging in a middle-class fantasy of achieving the illusion of a decent, meaningful existence – through community work and free schools and so on – in the midst of a repressive, brutal society. Have you more or less accepted the validity of that critique in retrospect?*

MARTELL: Well, there's a sense in which her criticism was tangential to what I was concerned about. But I've also changed my mind about a lot of things since those days. I agree entirely with Marjaleena's analysis of the way in which poor people are organized against the working class, and I never disagreed with it at the time. My experience in those days was not a counter-culture experience in any sense – it never was – I was simply enjoying the hell out of teaching literature to street kids and really my analysis didn't go much further than that. I was concerned about the kind of situation it would be nice to teach literature to street kids in – with asides about the oppressiveness of the corporations. I also believed then that neighbourhood organizing, done properly and not in any sense in opposition to labour organizing, would have an equal place to organizing in the work-place; and I no longer think that's true. The equality, that is. I think the *basic* political organizing has to happen primarily at the work place and that the most fundamental thing to do in this country is to build a strong and militant Canadian union centre. Which is not to say that neighbourhood organizing shouldn't continue. Only that it should be fused with a larger labour movement.

MYERS: *And still with a strong emphasis on decentralization and community involvement.*

MARTELL: That's right, but that has to come within a strong working-class movement built on the workplace.

MYERS: *Did that mean that you lost your faith that a whole lot of little things would come together into something significant?*

MARTELL: Yes. There's no question that people who are doing community work ought not to be discouraged from doing it and those people who are working seriously in the schools ought not to be discouraged; but they also must be encouraged to link up their efforts with building up a powerful working-class movement in Canada based around Canadian unions. On their own they'll remain powerless. You only have to look at the gutting of downtown Toronto; as things stand, it won't be stopped by groups like CORRA.

MYERS: *Just going back to your own development then, from those early articles till now, were you a socialist to start with?*

MARTELL: Yes, I was a socialist to start with.

REPO: Starting from where?

MARTELL: I would say that very early on in the magazine we were utopian socialists.

REPO: We were socialists in a very poetic way.

MARTELL: Socialists in a very poetic way. All right, we weren't Marxists, but we were anti-capitalist. Simply, we were utopian socialists. If somebody told us we were utopian socialists, we vehemently denied it. We said, "Of course, we're practical people." We believed in revolution. We knew there had to be a transition period between capitalism and socialism, but that was for somebody else, however, to concern themselves with. Not us.

REPO: We were doing these little models for others to imitate.

MARTELL: That's right. But my own development towards a Marxist position began with utopian socialism. I mean what it really came down to in practice, was a kind of practical anarchism developing in communal situations – whether in schools or co-ops or city residents' associations or what have you – and seeing that get beaten, watching it get wiped out. You see that what you consider to be reasonable arguments clearly make no difference. All the Jane Jacobs in the world aren't going to alter things. That kind of delicate and very human analysis of how nice it would be if only we were all reasonable, and we understood that cities are intricate social webs when they work, and we learn to preserve our local butcher because we know all the great things he does to keep the neighbourhood together, all that keeping of keys and confidences. It's very fine, and it's really true. We have a local butcher who does just that thing, but we know damn well that six months from now he won't be there – he's going to be out on his ass, when our local developer moves in. The utopian awareness, of what a great scene a city could be, is not enough. It's very important to keep in the back of your head all the time, because that finally is what you're fighting for; but you must deal with the organization of the mass of the people, the working class in the society, that will make that world a practical reality over a long period of time. You realize that the residents' groups get cleaned because they have no base, they simply have no handle on society. And if you're concerned about pushing back corporate capitalism, gradually your position starts to shift as you start realizing that you have to make a class analysis, that the only people who will move the society are the working class, who have power of the means of production.

REPO: I still believed then that the middle class was actually essential to movement in a way I don't see it as being central now. I was still under Marcuse's influence.

MARTELL: Marcuse was very influential.

REPO: For George and me more than for Bob, I think.

MARTELL: Marcuse put together for us Freud and Marx in a whole new way, a very important step for people in the middle class. But let me stress here that my teaching in the city was not, initially, a counter-culture scene at all – I was a pushy gang leader, for Christ sake. By the time we got the Point Blank building, it had started to become a counter-culture institution, but in my basement it was me and eight or nine kids. I was fairly tough about them working at reading and writing – if they didn't do a certain amount of work, then they got out. It wasn't a Bereiter approach; it was much more Sylvia Ashton-Warner, *firm* Sylvia Ashton-Warner. But finally, when it came to the crunch, what I was offering working-class kids was the option to be a bourgeois artist, and I got one – a real good one – who may in fact be much better than that. Right now he's made two very good films and certainly has prospects of making many more. But, for most, I didn't offer anything long-term – there was no sense in which they became educated and moved into a larger working-class movement.

DAVIS: The tools that you gave them were not useful in that sense.

MARTELL: That's right, that's right! They couldn't use that reading in the best sense. I never, of course, encouraged mobility – I always encouraged them to fight against it, but. .

Another inadequacy in our position was that it just did not deal with the national question; it was very much a North American analysis. Once you take that 49th parallel seriously, then your whole framework starts to shift.

MYERS: *This, of course, has been another major change in the attitude of* This Magazine, *from a continentalist position to a nationalist stance. I came across something Bob wrote, about* This Magazine *and the Ontario Department of Education having at least one thing in common: that the basic questions of education in North America transcended political boundaries. . .*

DAVIS: Did I say that?

MYERS: *And George, in his article in* Close the 49th Parallel, *seemed to take the view that the country had been lost and, although we should retain what independence we could, essentially we were all Americans and must work out American solutions to our problems.*

DAVIS: Actually, the most outrageous example of our continentalism was that book [*This Book is About Schools*] published by Pantheon.

REPO: No, I don't think that was the most outrageous.

DAVIS: I think it sold for $9.00 in Canada and $7.00 in the States.

MARTELL: It was four years ago and no Canadian publisher would touch it with a ten-foot pole, and this American house came to us and said, "We'd really like to publish your book and not only that we'll print a lot of pictures and have a great design and. . ."

REPO: Actually that book obviously should have been published in the United States. It was very much a continental book and that's why it should get a continental circulation.

DAVIS: That makes it a positive virtue!

MARTELL: My only justification at public meetings to people who brought that up, you know, was to say, "Well, personally we didn't make any money on it. It all went to a good cause – using Yankee money to keep a Canadian magazine alive." Not a very strong position, I'm afraid.

REPO: We felt much more North American then.

MARTELL: Well, it wasn't just that I felt North American. I was deeply pessimistic about the potential of various groups in this country to get it together in time to develop an independent socialist state.

REPO: And *Quebec* has been a major thing in giving people a second thought of the possibility of independence.

MYERS: *What is your view of what has happened in Quebec? Was the initial rise to national consciousness amongst the working class, or was the vanguard essentially middle-class, the university student and so on? Are there useful parallels for English-speaking Canada?*

REPO: We didn't follow it as closely as we should have, but I think that two things happened at the same time. First there was this kind of a cultural nationalism that, of course, found expression in the universities and in the arts in the late Sixties; and then they also had an indigenous union movement. Unlike the rest of Canada, they had this powerful Quebec union movement which was as powerful as the international unions in Quebec.

MYERS: *Whether or not it was radical?*

REPO: It wasn't radical, it was reactionary. It was organized by the clergy and it was, in fact, set up at first by Duplessis to discourage the international unions, because it would be a movement that he could handle. But it turned out, because it was a nationalist movement, when it grew into the CNTU, it could respond to the local situations faster than the Canadian labour movement in general. Therefore, it grew and developed and became political and sophisticated in a way the rest of the labour movement did not. It definitely now has a working-class base and orientation, but it was bourgeois nationalism first, it had the universities and the teachers.

MYERS: *Looking at the rest of the country, would you say we have anything like that degree of bourgeois national consciousness, let alone an indigenous labour movement?*

MARTELL: No, of course not. How much we have is what's hard to come to grips with. How important the nationalist question is or Robin Matthews' emphasis on the revolution of the mind, which with the cultural question really opens people up to the socialist question, is very difficult to say. It happened in Quebec. There's no question that for many people the clear logic of nationalism leads to socialism. With Mel Watkins, for example, that was clearly the process. That was the case with the forerunners of the CNTU – they were a nationalist, pro-Duplessis union that gradually, as the logic of the nationalist question in Quebec became clear to them, became socialists.

MYERS: *Isn't it likely, however, that our governments will take some action on cultural matters as a cover for doing nothing on the political and economic fronts?*

MARTELL: But each time they do it, it hurts them, finally. The cultural question is always explosive in a colonized country. So the more Canadian publishers supported, for example, the better.

REPO: It has beneficial fallout effects irrespective of what the government's intention may be, say, to cool the people down.

MARTELL: Because the Canadian question is clear. If you say "I'm a Canadian nationalist", you *have* to be an anti-imperialist. It's two sides of the same coin. Which means you have to be against corporate capitalism because it's almost entirely controlled from the United States. I mean, you're just stuck with an immediate set of allegiances once you've said you are a nationalist. We really don't have an option to be bourgeois nationalists.

MYERS: *Along with the clear shift to a socialist and a nationalist position, you also seemed to be becoming more hopeful of effective political action on the left in Canada. Although you are sceptical of the NDP's commitment to major social change, you seemed to think that the Canadian tradition of a respectable party on the left offered some chance for it to move in a more radical direction. Do you still think this after seeing what has happened to the Waffle, in Ontario at least?*

MARTELL: Well, I don't really think the Waffle is serious – that's my intuition, anyway.

REPO: I don't think you know the Waffle well enough even to say that. I think that's really unfair because we haven't examined them with the kind of care necessary.

DAVIS: But if you start to be a little more optimistic about an independent socialist movement, it would have to be based on masses of the working class, and that's the critical question about the Waffle. They don't seem to have taken that seriously. That's the difference between looking at them and looking at what has happened in Quebec – it has depth.

REPO: But there are a lot of people involved. I did an interview with Mel Watkins and, at the time, I spent some time with Waffle people. My feeling was that they were *very aware* of where they had to move, they were very interested and very concerned and very determined to become a working class-oriented organization. But the struggle to stay within the NDP was the key to their strategy. That was so all-consuming, with their jobs and other things and they just found it very difficult to have time for goals because the NDP had been purging them for the past six months. And you have to realize that it's to the extent that it did make these forays into the working-class areas that it made itself an enemy of the international unions; that it's because of the big meeting in Windsor, with all those workers, and a number of other meetings with unionized workers, that it drew this tremendous animosity from the union bosses, and therefore made it impossible for Stephen Lewis to keep the union bosses and the Waffle in the party – not that he shed any tears at letting them go.

MYERS: *Well, if the possibility of the NDP moving left now seems unlikely to you, what alternatives remain?*

MARTELL: Much more thorough organizing on the left, then, is clearly the option, at the workplace and in the cities. The only option is to develop another political party on the left that is not a social democratic party, but a socialist party, and has a *Canadian* union base.

MYERS: *Do you see a long period now of splinter groups of one kind and another on the left?*

MARTELL: Yes, until a stronger Canadian union movement emerges. That's the first stage before any kind of political party of any serious strength can develop.

MYERS: *So you now see the nationalism issue as being really only effective in terms of working people, and splitting Canadian unions off from the internationals?*

REPO: It's not only that, although that's really an important part. Obviously national independence is also an important question at the universities and it's an important question in articulating the Canadian experience in the arts and so on. But where you have any muscle, it's going to be in the union movement.

MYERS: *Does the Council of Canadian Unions strike you as a serious enterprise in this direction?*

MARTELL: Oh, yes, it's clearly very serious. It's very small but it's principled. Some of the people who are its leaders have had thirty years of the most intense struggle to stay alive as *Canadian* unionists and socialists. Their integrity is beyond question. Whether or not the present form of the CCU is possible – whether it can hold – is another matter. The pressures at this time may be too great for it. But there's no doubt in my mind it's very serious.

DAVIS: The forces against it are very strong, of course, because their unions are generally more militant than most other unions, and so the Labour Relations Boards in various parts of the country try to make it much more difficult for their unions to get certified.

REPO: Also because the international unions have representatives on these Labour Relations Boards.

DAVIS: It's growing slowly in the West, partly by the traditional Canadian patterns, that militancy comes from the West first. The Waffle strategy for Canadian labour has looked good on paper but it never included saying openly that there's a need for a central structure. It seems to me that there is a clear need for a Canadian union structure.

MYERS: *Are you still interested in the left in the United States?*

MARTELL: No. That is to say, I'm still interested in them as brothers and sisters who live in a different country. We may also, at some later stage of this country's development, require their help.

REPO: They might require ours too.

MARTELL: And who knows, they might require our help. At any rate, obviously *This Magazine,* while it's become a nationalist journal, is also an international journal. We care very much that the American left is strengthened because we consider them comrades, but we now understand that their experience is of fairly limited use to us.

REPO: And it's clear to us now that the strategies might be quite different in Canada and the United States regarding social changes.

MARTELL: If you're an American, you can hardly be a nationalist. You're the imperial centre, you know.

REPO: And your attitude towards the state will be different too because you don't want to strengthen the American state if you're an American radical whereas there might be some arguments for a Canadian nationalist to strengthen the Canadian state.

MYERS: *In a recent issue of* This Magazine *you printed an appeal to teachers to write, under a pseudonym if necessary, about what their jobs and hassles were like. You said that* This Magazine *had concluded, from the experience of the last six years, that there was "no alternative to the public schools and that all our energies must go into changing that system." Finally you stated your conviction that teachers must be part of a broadly based left-wing coalition, uniting all the working people of Canada. Do you think teachers are likely to respond favourably to these notions?*

DAVIS: Well, that remains to be seen, doesn't it?

REPO: The school is the work place for the teacher.

MARTELL: We're saying to the teachers, "Join your allies – your only serious allies are working men and women in this country."

DAVIS: The teachers in Quebec, why do they now say they're workers like the rest?

MARTELL: Well, not all of them say they're workers – the leadership doesn't and a very substantial minority say they are, a powerful minority. There's no formed opposition to it yet, there has been no real backlash, which means a great deal. They really have taken a commanding lead in the development of teacher organization. But clearly the Quebec teachers' rise to consciousness came considerably later than the CNTU rise to consciousness and it built on that. The union movement provided a whole climate, a substantial shift of political structures. A new power base was formed to which teachers could then ally themselves.

REPO: Also the issue of nationalism was central. The Quebec teachers were and are heavily separatist.

MYERS: *But do you see teachers in the rest of the country as being in any sense in a similar position or similar frame of mind as the Quebec teachers?*

MARTELL: Well, of course, somebody who's organizing the teachers is organizing on the faith that somebody else is organizing the workers. But you can't ignore them, they are a massive constituency – 275,000 professional teachers in this country. And half of the provincial budget, for God's sake, and then doubled by municipal taxes. Many are also very angry, you know, and despairing when you scratch the surface.

REPO: But they're mostly angry about taking bloody courses, and what can you do with that? Most of the time they're not that displeased with their job, but certainly they're *not* pleased with their power.

MARTELL: Well, we'll see. That's what it's going to hang on – how alienated those teachers are – how much will-power does it take to have to go into that classroom, to keep order, and to see themselves and the kids die a little more each day. Ten years ago who would have believed the C.E.Q?

REPO: I've taught teachers who came from working-class homes. They've done better than their fathers, with a lot of struggle, their family is proud of them, they're sort of proud of themselves. It could be nicer in many ways, but they're not complaining too much about the job. It's a much better job than their father had or their brothers and sisters have. They do hate these bloody courses they have to take. I guess that's when I get them angriest, talking about these courses.

DAVIS: I am finding my own reaction to teachers interesting now that I am teaching some of those courses. Two years ago I would have been very upset by those stylistic things – they all seem so straight in their demeanour and style and so on. But in approaching the school system and society very differently than I did then, I am really not so concerned about that, and I find them more open than I would have expected then – in fact, for example, they are quite sympathetic to a class analysis approach.

MYERS: *Have there been any significant changes in the regular public school system over the past decade?*

MARTELL: No, there's been no significant change in the system. In my judgment, the people who run the corporations and the government understood the direction of the economy in the early 1960's, at kind of an instinctive level – I don't know to what extent they understood it analytically. They knew that they had to have some place to socialize and stratify all these people who were going to have no place in the economy or very low level white collar jobs. So they introduced that massive expansion of the technical and vocational system, increasing the dead end schools in every respect. And I think that what we're now seeing is the development of that basic decision.

MYERS: *What then was Hall-Dennis – empty rhetoric?*

MARTELL: No, Hall-Dennis, in my judgment, was a justification for the techniques used in those vocational and technical schools. A system responds, a system has a certain logic. What Hall-Dennis, in fact, does – with all that incredibly banal bullshit about the whole child, in a situation which is clearly oppressive to any kind of human wholeness, conveying the message that children should learn at their own speed – means they have no human standards. It is an advanced form of liberalism, which always has no notion of what human nature is, no sense of social or personal destiny. Their key intellectual statement, right in the centre of the report is from Heraclitus – something about "All is flux." No, I remember, something like: "Life is movement and repose is death." The Hall-Dennis people helped clear the way for the development of Special Education – that's *the* growing, powerful section of the Toronto Board for example. I think you'll see in the next ten years a great many of the Board bureaucrats, the top administrators, will come out of the Special Education Branch because those are the people who really have their hands on the major new mode of social control that will be operating in this country.

REPO: That gets back to my original interest in the role of social work in adjustment and counselling. An even more major part of the school system will be devoted to this kind of adjustment.

MARTELL: Yes. For many there are no jobs. And their number will increase.

DAVIS: I want to add something about what that means to the wealthy kids because that's very important. The school system is changing enough for them, in ways that are suitable, in the direction that corporate capitalism is growing. Their opposition is silenced by the Hall-Dennis kind of reform.

Society needs more flexibility now on the top level and it gets it within the school system. Those kids get more options – because we need to have a more flexible kind of thinking person that can move back and forth through the top jobs now. You also get spawnings of free schools within the system to drain other kinds of potential middle-class opposition.

MYERS: *Well where do you all go from here then? Bob is no longer at Everdale or an editor of* This Magazine. *Right?*

DAVIS: That's right. When I decided to stop being an editor, it wasn't because of any prime disagreement with George and Satu. I think if I had wanted to go on writing and having a magazine, I would probably have wanted it to be more of a popular one, but I wouldn't have been capable of doing that right now. But there's not that kind of basic disagreement – some people have said that those of us that left were still counter-culture freaks and the ones that stayed were hard-line Marxists. For me it was rather that I wanted to have time to think about general economic and political questions and not to spend so much time thinking particularly about schools. I've been connected since last August with the Sussex Day Care Centre. Since April we've been involved in a 24-hour-a-day occupation of another campus building which we're operating as a second day-care centre. This was after eight months of fruitless negotiation with the University of Toronto where it displayed its usual outrageous disregard for community concerns or housing or whatever. Anyway, this has several of the features of the counter-culture experience I'm familiar with and which I think still have a contribution to make in the political struggle I now believe in. I think there are certain counter-culture groups and institutions that can serve a useful vanguard purpose in certain limited struggles in limited ways, but I also am convinced that certain features of the counter-culture will be necessary to any serious, working-class, revolutionary struggle.

MYERS: *I take it, from the things we've been talking about, that with Satu and George* This Magazine *will continue to interest itself in education, but will become more seriously concerned with political issues on the left, particularly the Canadian independence question and developments on the labour front?*

REPO: Well, we're very much in a transition phase at the moment – in six months we'd be able to tell you much more definitely where we are and where we're going. The struggle is clearly going to be bigger than we thought. At the same time, we've learned a lot, you know. By being more politically involved we take the chance of losing the magazine, but if anything I become less cynical. Which is astonishing considering how many times we've been wrong. Anyway, we think that now we should move in the directions we've been talking about tonight – we haven't done it yet, you know. But from our past errors we've concluded that that's where we must go. Two years from now, when you interview us again, we'll tell you how it worked out!

MARTELL: Well, I'll tell you if it doesn't work, we're in real trouble.

REPO: We're always in trouble.

Those Who Can't Teach…

Eric S. Hillis

A number of fads have hit education in the last decades, and like the prediction that would provide us all with helicopters in our backyards by this year, few have come to fruition. A great deal of time and, more particularly, money have been expended in the search for improvements in education. At the risk of over-simplifying, these fads could be placed on a continuum ranging from thing-oriented solutions to people-oriented solutions. The "thing" solutions were the first to appear because of their appeal to a gadget-loving society. In this first wave of educational change, schools were inundated with increasingly more sophisticated audio-visual machinery. So much so that teachers had to be calmed by being told that the new items were adjuncts to, not replacements for, the classroom teacher. The promise of new and improved education as a result of the introduction of projectors, recorders and a variety of media materials never materialized. Critics suggested that the failure of education to improve immediately and appreciably as a result of the infusion of "modern" techniques could be traced to either the inability of the traditional system to cope with the new approaches demanded by the new materials, or, perhaps, the inability of the teachers themselves to change their techniques.

This gave rise to the second generation of educational solutions that were more pupil and curriculum oriented. These could be traced, in part, from the new technology as traditional subjects were programmed and packaged in media kits. Now the position of the teacher became more uncertain, and even more assurances were required. And again the promised benefits did not materialize on a readily identifiable scale. It should be noted that the value of the above developments is not denied, merely that the expectations held out for them far exceeded what could reasonably be expected.

Successive fads and successive disillusionments forced an examination of more basic concerns, and as the more thoughtful turned from technologically oriented solutions, they turned to the nature of the schools themselves. The re-examination of the school system saw the beginnings of the body of writing that called for the "de-schooling" of education, and the replacement of the traditional public school with a more flexible "free" school. (It is more accurate to term this a "popularization" than a beginning, for the concept of the "free school" can be traced back at least fifty years to A. S. Neill.) These alternatives to the public school system have flourished in isolated instances, and have been viable alternatives for some students. However, those who doubted their universal viability were not surprised at a recent statement by the editors of *This Magazine is About Schools* conceding that, "If there's anything we've learned over the last six years, it's that there is no alternative to the public schools, and that all our energies must go into changing that system."

The recent popularity of teacher education appears to be the next phase in this sequence of analysis. Given the evidence that technology cannot exist as an educational innovation in isolation, that the new alternative schools are solutions only for the few, and given the fact that education can no longer count on unlimited support from the public dollar, the logical next step is a re-examination of school personnel – the teacher and how he gets there.

The same danger exists for this analysis as existed for the previous bandwagons. The supporters of the new approach may create expectations that far exceed what can reasonably be expected of new programs for teacher preparation. While a re-examination of the process that claims to prepare a teacher is necessary and useful, there is no guarantee that it will produce a solution. Indeed, the very fact of the re-examination may create situations that make it difficult for teacher education to succeed.

After many years of existence, teacher education has achieved a current prominence primarily as the result of the failure of other perceived panaceas. To place the responsibility for improving education on teacher education alone is to exacerbate the mistakes of the past. For, in a number of ways, teacher education seems a very unlikely path to salvation. Traditionally, in Canada as elsewhere, it has been conducted in an atmosphere of governmental regulation, university misconception, and public disdain. In large measure the first two elements have created the third.

* * *

The effect of governmental regulation has been mixed. While the practice does provide a standard of competence for teachers in a province, it does this at the expense of a monotonous similarity among programs. Even worse, the regulations have become, in many cases, an excuse for inactivity because of the constraints assumed by faculties of education. For the educator really interested in innovation, these restraints are often more apparent than real.

Underlying this practice of having provincial governments act as the licensing agency for the profession is the basic premise that one can identify standards of performance for teachers. However, since teaching does not have a performance base which is as easily identifiable as it is for the traditional professions of medicine and law, the premise may be a bad one. There is, for example, no demonstrable correlation between the sorts of things required by provincial teacher licensing agencies and the sorts of skills that teachers see as necessary. This is not so much a reflection on the certification requirements as it is of the fact that there is no adequate descriptive analysis for the act of teaching. Thus, antagonism to the whole process of teacher education results from the apparent irrelevance of the standards set for programs.

The universities' attitudes to teacher education have been coloured by the fact that the offering of discrete professional training for the beginning teacher is a recent historical development. In a sense, it could be said that teacher education has returned to the university, but the *licentia docendi* granted by the mediaeval church and university was evidence of an academic preparation. The body of knowledge which was to become teacher education as we understand it developed, for the most part, outside the university. Such contemporary programming still carries with it the stigma of normal schools and teachers' colleges, even though these institutions are rapidly disappearing. If present trends in Canada continue, all teacher education will take place on university campuses within the next few years.

The move to put teacher education on the university campus springs from a variety of widely, and strongly, held beliefs. The most popular of these is the belief that an isolated institution, devoted solely to the preparation of teachers, is bad because of its narrowness. It does not give the prospective teacher access to a variety of academic and occupational outlooks. The argument that such institutions are restrictive is hard to deny, but one must ask if the move to a university campus offers a solution. Geography is not the only factor that gives rise to isolation, and the move to the campus may simply exchange one set of problems for another. It is apparent in cases where teachers' colleges have moved to university campuses that the new faculties have not been readily accepted into the university community.

Perhaps the misconception about teacher education most widely held in the university concerns its very nature. The member of a faculty of education has little doubt that there is an identifiable body of knowledge which, when packaged, can be termed teacher education. Such a faculty member has been exposed to this sort of training and finds it acceptable. The traditional university "academic" on the other hand, teaches quite happily without such training and tends to see teacher education as being carried on at the expense of a more useful and intensive academic preparation. To the university academic there is about as much relationship between teacher education and the education of a teacher as there is between a venetian blind and a blind Venetian.

To some extent, general public antipathy to teacher education springs from the same roots as the university's attitude. The general public has been exposed more to teachers than to any other class of professional and this familiarity has bred a certain contempt. Further, studies indicate that the esteem of practising teachers for the institutions where they received their professional education exists in barely measurable quantities. Even in programs where newness or novelty might have been expected to enhance student attitudes, one tends to find a basic dissatisfaction. Many of the reasons for this dissatisfaction stem from the fact that the programs of preparation offer solutions to problems as yet unperceived by the student, and are further distorted by a context that misunderstands the basic purposes of that education.

There are a variety of other problems that have characterized teacher education in this country. Because of the perceived low social status of teaching there is some evidence that less able candidates are attracted to it than to more lucrative or prestigious occupations. There is a very real problem in adequately and appropriately staffing teacher education faculties in a context where, on the one hand – the university's – academic qualifications are paramount, and, on the other – the school system's – practical experience is regarded as vital. And the list goes on.

Despite these many and daunting problems, and bearing in mind the dangers of being carried away on yet another educational bandwagon, the recognition that teacher education must be of central concern to anyone seriously interested in the improvement of the public school system is a very welcome development. The rhetoric about the key importance and crucial significance of the teacher's role has always been plentiful, but usually educational "reformers" have preferred to evade that reality by tinkering with reorganized time-tables, shiny technology, or brightly packaged curriculum kits. Recently, however, there has been a spate of important reports on teacher preparation and these are generating interest beyond the confines of purely professional groups. A short, and biased, list of these would include B. O. Smith's *Teachers for the Real World,* John McDonald's *The Discernible Teacher,* the report of the University of British Columbia's Committe on the Future of the Faculty of Education (COFFE), *Teacher Education: Perseverance or Professionalism* by the Committee on Teacher Education at the University of Prince Edward Island (TEPOP), and the literature surrounding the development of a number of experimental teacher education programs funded by the United States Office of Education. These latter programs have been perceptively analysed by, among others, S. C. T. Clarke of the University of Alberta.

In Canada, a great deal of discussion was generated by these writings, particularly the COFFE report. This statement, regarded in tandem with previous developments at Simon Fraser University, was the first fresh, comprehensive look at teacher education in Canada. Along with McDonald's *Discernible Teacher,* the COFFE report has provided a sound basis for further analysis, and the influence of these documents can be clearly seen in the subsequent P.E.I. report.

This latter report characterizes one of the more interesting developments in teacher education – the involvement of persons outside the field of teacher education. In light of the fact that contacts between teacher education facilities and the rest of the university have been minimal and sporadic, this is a most desirable tendency. While one suspects that such coalitions start with the belief that given close contact each side will convert to the other's view, nonetheless the result tends to be a product and approach that draws strength from a broader and more varied base.

Most of the contemporary writing on teacher education starts with the assumption that the programming will be offered in a university context. With this basis, the discussions tend to centre on sequence and content of courses, and more recently on the concept of the field experience or internship. Predictably, much time has been spent in devising ways in which teacher education can be offered in a university environment without allowing the process of adapting to university structures to dictate the function of the new programs.

A variety of approaches have been discussed, ranging from the skill-oriented perspective of some of the model programs funded in the United States, to a more casual academic-professional integration advocated by the Prince Edward Island report. The COFFE study tends more towards the former approach of modular programming with specified objectives. It should be noted that, throughout the literature, it is evident that the traditional course of one or two semesters duration is being discarded. Programs are being constructed around units of work or experience that can vary in length with the performance of the students.

The concept of an internship has also received a great deal of attention. The one constant in the many varieties of programming offered or proposed has always been the field experience, primarily because it has enjoyed almost unanimous praise from students as being the most useful component of their preparation. It has been suggested that in some cases the inclusion of an internship has sprung from the belief that if a little is good, more is better. This is not quite fair, however, for the internship concept is appreciably different from the model school, demonstration lesson approach that often appeared in normal schools, and is a qualitative improvement over the scatter-shot practice teaching of more recent history. Basically, the internship concept is an improvement because it provides a more realistic block of time in the schools, and if carefully implemented can also provide a better integration of course work and practical experience than does the practice of placing students in classrooms for isolated days or parts of days.

Notwithstanding the fact that the internship is a traditional and borrowed concept, its introduction into teacher education programming on a broad scale is the first step towards creating more permanent and beneficial bonds between the institutions that prepare teachers and the schools which will employ them. While it may be regarded as a peripheral benefit at the moment, this channel of contact and communication that opens up with the closer cooperation of school and university by mutual participation in the internship period may become the most important development in teacher education.

Not only has the analysis of teacher education resulted in new working relationships being established inside the university and with schools, but it is also apparent that a variety of outside agencies are becoming involved in the planning and preparation of programs. This is all the more remarkable because of the insular way in which teacher education has functioned in the past. However, in these new expanded relationships lies the potential for conflict.

In the community, there is a strong feeling that public participation in schools and faculties of education is necessary. The hypothesis that children must be exposed to a wide range of people and experiences during their education is unchallengeable. Traditionally, the school has tended to leave this element of a child's education to outside agencies. Thus some critics have drawn an effective distinction between "education" and "schooling." This distinction led William Carr for example to see the school as "An Island Apart" and comment that:

> Many schools are like little islands set apart from the mainland of life by a deep moat of convention and tradition. Across this moat there is a drawbridge which is

lowered at certain periods during the day in order that part-time inhabitants may cross over to the island in the morning and back to the mainland at night. Why do these young people go out to the island? They go there in order to learn how to live on the mainland. When they reach the island they are provided with a supply of excellent books that tell about life on the mainland. They read these books diligently, even memorizing parts of them. Then they take examinations on them.

Current developments are attempting to reduce or eliminate the gap, in part by encouraging the participation of a variety of individuals in regular classroom work. While this is a commendable and desirable trend, it can create difficulties for the traditional participants in public education. It is difficult to envisage teachers, as a professionally separate group, encouraging the participation of non-professionals in the schools, particularly at a time when the supply of teachers exceeds the demand. There is a distinct possibility that such a situation will lead to rather more traditional solutions, rather than ones that tend to encroach further upon a beleaguered profession.

To take it one step further, the two naturally antagonistic trends of professional self-protection and community involvement could lead to a basic division between two of the agencies most interested in improving education. Parents and community-minded individuals cannot help but feel rebuffed if their offers of assistance are seen as implied criticism of the work of the teacher, and as a threat to the teacher's security. The teachers' organizations, on the other hand, will find it extremely difficult and perhaps impossible to encourage any trend, however desirable, that tends to reduce the number of teachers presently employed. The compromise that will come from this will probably be the same limited participation of the past. Any minor modifications that result will be all the less acceptable because of the increased expectations of the other agencies. The conflict itself will force further examination of the preparation of teachers and a predictable outcome would be a reduction in the importance of the teacher as teacher.

One cannot help but note that a great many of the changes suggested for teacher education increase the length of time required to prepare a teacher. This is reasonable if, in fact, education is as complex and as important a topic as we would be led to believe. However, quantity must not be confused with quality. There must be more to a "new" program for teachers than just another semester or two and a longer period of exposure to the schools. To be significantly better, it must be significantly different. Programs must not simply perpetuate practices that have the authority of long usage, they must look to qualitative change. As B. O. Smith noted,

> *No matter how effective training procedures may be or how fruitful conceptions of learning or teaching may be in generating ways of conducting instruction, teaching will not be improved if the skills taught in teacher education programs have no greater influence upon pupils education than the skills teachers ordinarily use.*

Whatever the results, it is clear that teacher education across the country is becoming firmly situated in the universities. At some places, indeed, it is even seen as making a contribution to a general university education and undergraduates actually enrol in Bachelor of Education courses and programs for their educational quality as much as for their professional necessity. Generally the length of time required for teacher education programs is becoming equivalent to other programs offered in the university. There are indications, too, that the universities are more interested in their own teaching programs and techniques and are, therefore, more sympathetic to and interested in the concerns of teacher education faculties.

The regulation of teacher education by governmental agencies shows signs of becoming less authoritarian. A desirable trend would be for provincial departments of education to set the broadest possible standards for the preparation of teachers, and allow B.ED. programs to be evaluated by cooperative groups involving all interested parties. As the prime minister noted in a slightly different context, "the government has no place in the B.ED.-rooms of the nation."

Another factor which should be noted is that there is apparently an over-supply of teachers at the present time. This creates a host of problems in the realm of teacher selection and evaluation, but it does enable programs that have been concerned with the quantity of their output to deal with qualitative questions about programs. The fact that teacher education programs can more than meet the demand of the school system not only allows an examination of the process of preparation, it makes it imperative.

Education generally, and educators in particular, have long smarted under the widely held old saw: "Those who can, do; those who can't, teach; those who can't teach, teach teachers." While the teacher education of the past may not have stood up under close examination, the broad spectrum of interest now being shown in teacher education creates the potential for it to be appreciably better in the future. The involvement of a variety of persons with a common interest in the improvement of education will enable teacher education to identify and serve the needs felt by the communities it serves. This is inestimably better than basing programs on aims, purposes and needs too often identified by the teacher educator working in isolation.

While one must beware the fact that the re-examination of teacher education may be just a fad, springing from the failure of other educational fads, even this attention is better than the indifference of the past. The most optimistic are those who can be heard muttering under their breaths, ". . . those who can't teach, practice law or medicine."

Goodbye Chips, Hello Jean

David Beard

The last four decades of motion pictures have not attempted to change the image of the schoolmarm. She is a God-fearing, sexless, underpaid authoritarian, who, despite all difficulties, remains dedicated to her students. The male in the profession has not fared quite so well. Often depicted as an out-of-touch, impotent martinet, he soon fell victim to his own foibles. On the whole, though, the teacher as a self-interested member of society did not interest the movie maker or the audience. The concept of the teacher as a person with limitations and some insurmountable problems was ignored in favour of the traditional image. Two recent exceptions emerged in the late Sixties.*The Prime Of Miss Jean Brodie* and *Rachel, Rachel* suggested that not all female teachers were blue stockings, at least not quite all. The present decade has yet to produce a film that reflects the developing crisis in the school, in the teacher and/or their inter-relationship with society.

In examining the movies of the past four decades it is possible to realize that the social values of those decades are still cherished by the audiences and the movie makers. The traditional view of the teacher is best seen in *Good-bye Mr. Chips,* the Robert Donat version made in 1939. Lindsay Anderson's *If. . .* killed off this Victorian relic. Hollywood revived him in an embalmed version just thirty years later in 1969. Social values bring money to the box-office.

If. . . challenged the traditional value placed upon teachers.

The one value or force the producers placed in the films of that period was the conflict the teacher experienced when she was trying to accomplish "good" in the life of her students, despite the "bad" administration. The teacher often accomplished a "little good". This was appreciated by the one sensitive student. Then the teacher had to pay for her "little triumph" over the forces of ignorance. The price? Her job! And, like the stranger who came into town and took the tin star to save the town from itself, the teacher left to look for Another Dawn in which the same thing would happen all over again. The pupil remained, young and bewildered. "What strange ways adults have," she said to herself. The teacher, older and not much wiser, gazed into the sunset and asked why institutions had to be manned by the certificated and not the sensitive. In the late sixties *If...* questioned the system. It retained the public image of the teacher but it presented a new image of the student. The last frame of this film revealed the new order standing on the ramparts of education. Not books, but guns were the tools of education. Here are the new teachers who are willing to instruct their elders. The film found support from the young. Did it reflect changing social values?

In the past, several films attempted to show the teacher as a human being. In *Terms of Trial* ('62) the teacher (male) is accused by a girl student of immoral conduct. *The Children's Hour* ('62) presented the teacher as a victim of gossip. In the classic, *Blue Angel* ('30), the teacher succumbs to his vanity. *Inherit The Wind* ('60) depicted the teacher as a pawn in a political-religious-legal battle over the teaching of evolution in the classroom. The drama is developed in each film from the premise that the teacher has a traditional rôle assigned to him/her by society. Certain behaviour is demanded; getting involved with a female student, homosexuality, lust or imparting new ideas is not expected of the teacher. The audience willingly accepted the premise although for a certain time during the showing of the film it is possible for the audience to identify with the teacher's conflict. This identification did not involve an approval of the teacher's "crime". The denouement arrived. The scale of justice was balanced. The audience retired in the belief that justice had been served. Of course, they said, we need law and order – especially for teachers. After all they are in constant contact (the right sort) with the young. Besides they are only human.

Two short films became well known in the profession, *No Reason to Stay* (NFB) and *High School* (Wiseman, 1968, USA) Both films depict teachers in the worst possible light. Both are made in the documentary style. This contributes to the impact each film delivers. Both are relentless and both imply that there are no compensating benefits in the institutional situation. (The simplistic analysis a documenary can inflict upon an audience is causing its revival among political activists.) Black and white lends itself both philosophically and economically to the style, and to the subject. Every teacher is shown to be severely human and quite tragically ridiculous. The films fail to grant the teachers any dignity whatever. (The feeling is conveyed that they have none.) *No Reason to Stay* is melodramatic and simplistic. (Have you ever seen a more distressed mother? Can you believe she held a job in Toronto's great financial jungle?) Such melodrama might be defended on the grounds that the point of view is that of the adolescent. Yet we are expected to believe him. A scene in the film depicts a rather prissy male teacher who is ultimately, in fantasy, put before the firing squad. Prior to his demise the screenwriter captures a disturbing and believable tone of sarcasm, when the teacher belittles a student, a scene which is always cause for discussion when the film is shown. Teachers feel compelled to defend him with, "We are not all like that." or they justify his tone with, "If you had to put up with that sort all day, you'd do the same". *High School* and *No Reason to Stay* have something worth pointing out, although this does not mean that ultimately they have anything worth saying about teachers or about schools. Both films cause teachers to take untenable points of view. It has been obvious for some time that the alternatives to the education system and to the problems of learning do not lie within the power of the school or the teachers to solve. Yet these films suggest that teachers have "real" power; they neglect the possibility that the teachers are caught as the students are caught. The teacher will always appear in the poorest light when he or she is put in a no-man's land of education by society.

The image of the teacher as a lady has been amply supplied to the audience by Deborah Kerr. In *Black Narcissus* ('46) Deborah went off to India as a missionary. Her main concern was not education (as it turned out), but to keep the sexual forces at bay while carrying on the Christian work amid the natives. She failed. Later Deborah went to Hollywood where she made *The King and I* ('56). Again she ventured into the dark world of Siam (near India in the minds of movie goers). There she taught the Puritan virtues of holding the head erect, singing a happy tune and saying, "Shall we dance?" instead of "Shall we bed?" Only a governess and a lady could sustain the values of our English institutions in the face of the barbarians. *Tea and Sympathy* ('56) brought social awareness! At last Hollywood admitted that a teacher was capable of sexual response, but only under the most critical circumstances. Deborah's tuition extended to the bed of her young friend when he had severe doubts about his masculinity. In *The Innocents* ('61) she played a hysterical virgin who imagines all sorts of unnatural events. Deborah served the motion picture public faithfully in the image they loved – the teacher as a lady.

Other actresses have portrayed teachers (surely the most bizarre was Mae West as Flower Belle Lee in *My Little Chickadee* ('40) with W. C. Fields). Bette Davis played Lilly Moffat in *The Corn is Green* ('45). Miss Davis attempted to save a young man from the horrors of the Welsh mines by educating him and finally caring for his illegitimate child. (He won. She lost.) *Good-morning Miss Dove* ('55) saw Jennifer Jones in the title rôle – a female Mr. Chips. In 1967

Sandy Dennis played Sylvia Barrett in *Up the Down Staircase*. Sylvia overcame the bureaucrats in the ghettoes of New York. By the late Sixties the movies were willing to admit that the teacher was not all saint. Maggie Smith played Jean in *The Prime of Miss Jean Brodie* ('69).

On the brink of the Seventies the teacher, according to the movies, had heard of politics in relation to her job. Although still an authoritarian she had been granted a sex life. She was wise and silly at the same time. She was heir to human vanities. She taught from convictions although not quite the wisest ones. Best of all she was facing the reality of being fired and putting her pension in jeopardy. The Miss Doves who insisted that the student have a clean, white hanky pinned to the chest were dead. Gone was the teacher's "good-morning class"; the new atmosphere had the smell of battle. Jean Brodie almost killed off the old maid concept, as well as the lady schoolteacher complex. Jean had the hint of liberation. Unfortunately, there has not been a film to explore further the broken ground. At least Jean put the public image of a female teacher – a well-covered dry bone with feet at one end and lessons at the other – to rest.

Men teachers have been presented, in the main, as moths without wings. John Ford's *How Green was my Valley* ('41) has, as a minor character, a bullying school teacher. Because he caned a student he is roughed up by some of the men who escaped the advantages of the child's education. Michael Redgrave played the sour, acidic pedagogic teacher in *The Browning Version* ('51). In 1955 Glen Ford played Richard Dadier (Daddy-O) in *The Blackboard Jungle*. Dadier believed that the ghetto children would respond if the right method could be found. Laurence Olivier's teacher in *Term of Trial* ('62) lacked an understanding of the growth of his teen-age student. In *To Sir With Love* ('67), Sidney Poitier presented a sympathetic teacher who throws the books out when he realizes that his students will soon be on the labour market. He teaches them survival tactics. These lessons include How to Shop Wisely and How to Make a Salad! It is a nauseating, sentimental view of a teacher with a popular song, sung in the midst of departing student tears.

If. . . ('69) recalls the rebellious atmosphere of the French *Zéro de Conduite* ('33). The headmaster is depicted as chief moth. "Education," he comments after Matins, "in Britain is a nubile Cinderella sparsely clad and much interfered with." Stewart, who rides his bike through the hallowed hall, is arrogant. The chaplain who teaches mathematics is a sadist. The light of learning has failed to stir these wingless creatures. Several films attempted to cash in on the popularity of *If. . .*, but they failed to interest the audience. Student power against the establishment with drug takers and light shows thrown in for the "heads" (a showing of a film where the audience takes a little pot to improve the visual perception) had no validity. *Billy Jack* is the sleeper of the Seventies. Showing life at a u.s. version of Summerhill, students of ten years and up have been the film's main supporters. Billy Jack is an Indian and friend to the school. He is the "real" teacher in the film. In the years from 1941 to 1971 little has changed for the male teacher.

The motion picture is a force in society that shapes the individual's and the masses' concept of reality. Thus, it creates life styles for individuals and for mass expression. Perhaps the teacher can transcend the image assigned to him or her by the public as reflected in the motion picture. Movies are concerned with the drama of that contradiction – the mass vs. the individual. Perhaps, the militant teachers can force their issues through to the mass media. Inevitably this revolution will become the new orthodoxy in motion picture terms. It might just occur to the industry that holding a gun and threatening to change the system is just as oppressive as the authoritarian holding up a book and maintaining the system by legal requirements. The motion picture under present conditions has to be aware not of the equal evils, but of the ascendency most in favour with the public. The revolution or the orthodoxy will be the status quo at any given time. The prime concern of the motion picture industry is not to tell the truth, or to reflect social values at any given time, it is to make a profit. That profit can be made by reflecting social values at the expense of a professional class is unimportant to the industry and to the public. Audiences seek reinforcement of their cherished social values or prejudices. They are not entertained by the destruction of them.

Canadian Studies—Problems and Prospects

Albert Tucker

The contribution of education to a distinctive Canadian consciousness is largely accidental. Given the total control of provincial governments over education in Canada, with their bureaucratic supervision of curricula, it is remarkable that our schools produce in their graduates any sense at all of a shared national experience. This observation remains true despite the growing interest in Canadian Studies as a legitimate subject of concentration in the high schools and the universities.

At one extreme is the judgment published four years ago in Book II of the Report of the Royal Commission on Bilingualism and Biculturalism: "Canadian history as it is taught today tends to maintain and even strengthen cultural antagonisms." The commissioners were agreeing with briefs on the teaching of Canadian history which insisted that by bias and omission, "we are fostering cultural divisions and animosities in Canada." Specifically they stressed the differences between French and English textbooks on Canadian history. "In the French-language textbooks the dominant theme is the development and survival of French-Canadian society. . . In English-language textbooks the central theme is the establishment and survival of Canada as a political entity in North America."

Beyond these more intense and lingering differences are those which arise from provincial divisions generally. Bernard Hodgetts published the results of his National History Project in the same year as the B. & B. Report. His findings corroborated the dominance of the textbook as the central focus for the teaching of Canadian history in the classroom. Since then Hodgetts has gone on, with dedicated energy, to establish the Canada Studies Foundation. Its second annual report, released at the end of last March, points once again to the fragmented nature of our educational system.

As presently prescribed and taught, provincially designed Canadian Studies programs, for reasons that have been carefully analyzed in earlier documents of the Foundation, seldom give students a real appreciation of their total nation-wide environment or any sympathetic understanding of differing value systems, aspirations or views of Canada's future.

The direction being given to the Canada Studies Foundation by Walter Gordon and George Tomkins added to the initiative of Mr. Hodgetts and his bilingual secretariat, may yet produce valuable approaches and tools for study. Their kits on specific projects, their pamphlets, their films, and their inter-regional conferences of students could provide, over the next three years, a series of outlines for common understanding, for means of communications among teachers at a national level, which have not previously existed in the various educational systems of the country. The outcome is problematic. At the present time the rhetoric of the Foundation is impressive, but it outstrips any widespread knowledge of actual results.

Equally significant are two facts. The Foundation is, first of all, entirely the work of individuals acting effectively in a private, non-governmental capacity. Secondly, its projects will depend for their impact not only on their quality but on the eventual cooperation of officials and administrators who must sanction the ways in which innovation is incorporated into the system.

❊   ❊   ❊

This context of bureaucratic control, of administrative hierarchy and provincial divisions, helps to explain the continuing inchoate character of Canadian Studies in the schools generally. But it is not by any means the sole explanation. There are two others. One has to do with the universities and their influence; the other with the unique and fundamental differences over language and culture.

The liberal arts curricula of Canadian universities reflect the limitations of our combined inheritance from Britain and the United States. Knowledge is divided almost rigidly by discipline, the result of a positivist fragmentation in American higher education associated with the application of empirical assumptions about scientific method to the study of man in society. In their haste to match the highest North American standards, our universities have imitated this division-by-discipline all too readily. It was never done with much originality. The consequences are serious when attempts are now made to develop programs in Canadian Studies.

The integrity of the discipline, with its implicit structure, takes precedence over the coherence of a program that is pieced together from existing or newly created courses. At all of our universities we must start with a given and relatively fixed curriculum. At most, with few exceptions, the precedence of the discipline and its prescriptive right, have prevented a strong innovative base for Canadian Studies. They lack a core or synthesis of intellectual content which would conceptually unite a broad range of subjects. The Ford grant received by Trent University for its curriculum in Canadian Studies will stimulate a program already strong in talent and resources, but one that is essentially constituted from a wide variety of existing courses. Within a year, we hope, T. H. B. Symons will have completed his survey of Canadian Studies programs for the Association of Universities and Colleges of Canada, and we shall all know more about how far such programs extend and their effectiveness for students.

At the present time the advantage often lies with the high-school rather than the university teacher. If he is possessed of imagination and is not hidebound by distinctions of discipline the teacher at the level of the secondary school or the community college may well be free to devise his own interdisciplinary course of study, combining history, psychology, sociology, and geography in ways not open to the university professor, however flexible and experimental he may wish to be.

Teachers are becoming freer to develop these courses on their own initiative, but are receiving little encouragement or help from the universities. Few academics in university departments sustain genuine communication with those of their students who go on to teach. Where such contact exists it is generally at a sporadic local level, dependent on personality and interest. As a result, academic courses remain largely indifferent to the needs of the secondary-school classroom. Canadian Studies have not developed in the universities as central or even relevant to the training of teachers.

This gap of differing experiences and interests is apparent also in the lack of any national association of teachers of history, an organization that is badly needed if curricula and experiments in the classroom are to be discussed in a Canadian rather than solely in a provincial context. The Canadian Historical Association makes a gesture to teachers outside university history departments through its Committee on the Teaching of History, but few teachers are involved; the majority hardly know that the committee exists. The C.H.A. remains largely an association of academic faculty talking to themselves, with little awareness of the complex problems being faced by history teachers who are confronted by the continuous decline of history in the high-school classrooms. We have nothing in Canada that compares, for instance, with the Historical Association in England.

Assuming that Canadian history, in any case, will have to merge more intricately with subjects generally designated as "social science", what is still needed is a central forum on a national scale. There is at present no organization that would supply and communicate information, sustain a wideranging dialogue among teachers, and provide continuous, systematic contact between their needs and what the universities can offer. A most vital contribution to the whole discussion could well come from a national journal, on the model perhaps of the present *Canadian Journal of History and Social Science,* which is unfortunately suspect because it is based in Ontario.

* * *

With a professional, well-edited journal and a national association, agreement may yet be reached on the relationship in educational curricula between regional diversity and national identity. Such a realization would, however, have to surmount the barrier of language and culture. Part of the way to bring about English and French dialogue may lie in more effective translation of readings and tapes, so that anglophone and francophone students know at an early age the premises and biases inherent in the materials being studied by each. The curricula of secondary education may then become related in more meaningful ways to an earlier understanding of the fundamental differences in culture.

The fact that such understanding is still a parched and fragile plant suggests that as Canadians we have lacked the will to make education a vehicle of national identity. As institutions financed and directed by the State, the schools could inculcate a more sensitive understanding of national ideals, as they have for long inculcated democratic values.

But the task involves a continuous appreciation of the clear possibility that Canada will never achieve a political and cultural unity. In terms of nationhood, we shall always be in a process of becoming. There is, as Michel Brunet has said, "no permanent solution to the problem of French Canada and its collective aspirations." To satisfy self-determination in Quebec the best that we can hope for may be coexistence within a loose federal compromise.

That question, however, must enter fundamentally into more interdisciplinary programs of Canadian Studies, and it must be enriched by acknowledging that anyone who teaches such programs, at any level, should fully comprehend and be able to communicate in the French language. The challenge of language and of interdisciplinary study, together with the superb books and essays now being published in Canadian sociology, literature and history, could challenge the best talents we have in education. Our most gifted teachers should be encouraged to see Canadian Studies in a variety of programs as a prestigious core of the liberal arts, whether in secondary or post-secondary institutions.

Community Schools in Toronto: A Sign of Hope

Fiona Nelson

Much alarm has been generated of late by the thesis that "school is dead". Budget ceilings, rampant careerism and a trend towards the corporate management approach in education are all resulting in a most disordered state of affairs. Education, a public service, is increasingly acting to the disadvantage of its own clients. In this, it is merely following the course of its two companion bureaucracies, Health and Welfare. Taxpayer and client discontent with all of these services is growing apace. It is not surprising that a disgruntled citizenry objects to constantly being at the wrong end of a law of diminishing returns, but it is strangely self-destructive for education to have been made the focus of all the discontent. In refusing to pay the shot for education, government hurts the entire community, but perhaps no more so than the deadhand bureaucracy much of schooling has become.

It is no doubt characteristic of moribund bureaucracies to self-destruct, and there are those who would be delighted to hasten the process. To hear the newspapers tell it, the taxpayers would be better off to rid themselves of so wasteful an encumbrance. However, some recent developments in Toronto indicate that here, at least, school is very much alive and likely to become much more so. Brown School, Park, Oak St., Laneway, Kensington, Balmy Beach, Alpha, Contact and Seed and others are all becoming "community schools" in one sense or another. But a large question still remains and it asks what "community school" is and how does it differ from a conventional or "straight" (or dead?) school?

"Community schools" to anyone who does not take the community seriously, may mean anything from letting the Cubs and Brownies in after school to having the parents come in one night a year for serious chats about "marks". To those who have the numb sensation that somehow the electoral process has left them disfranchised, "community school" means something more than after-hours use of schools. To some it means community control, in the sense that the school "supplies" what some people "demand". To others it means community involvement, in the sense that parent groups cooperate actively with Board officials and trustees in the planning of schools or programs. Another common view is that community schools entail the use of parents and other non-certificated adults as volunteers in the classroom. However, these are all partial definitions because they do not as yet offer the defining characteristics of a *community* which will serve to distinguish the real article from the token gesture. No doubt the differtia (i.e. the peculiar features which distinguish various communities) are legion, and any number of them may be present even in a conventional school. But if the defining characteristics of *community* are not present, you do not have a community, and hence you do not have a community school.

The Ontario Ministry of Education has attempted to isolate these characteristics in its official definition, as follows:

> . . . *the school that becomes a community focus should do so because of a natural development rather than because of artificial forcing. For such a natural feeling of unity, there ought to be*:
> 1. *an expressed desire on the part of local citizens to utilize the school as a community resource;*
> 2. *a compact body of potential users within a reasonable radius of the school;*
> 3. *a large enough group of interested citizens to warrant*

the formation of a class or club;
4. the appropriate facilities in the school;
5. willing and capable leaders in both school and community.1

However, this definition fails for two important reasons. It has attempted to define community schools in terms of generalizations which cannot possibly cover all the characteristics of individual communities and community schools, as they have developed or are likely to develop. Worse still, this definition considers only community use of the existing facilities.

With all the forces which are affecting our schools, and with the variety of interpretations of community schools which are current, it might be well to examine the circumstances which prompted community action in several Toronto schools. From this sample it may be possible to draw some active principles. Perhaps too, they can offer some clues to the kind of definition which is needed to guide public policy in the days ahead.

           *   *   *

Brown School

Brown School is on the border of the "Republic of Rathnelly", an enclave of fairly prosperous houses in a north central location. This neighbourhood probably has a higher concentration of creative professionals than any other in Canada. It has a stable population – the children at Brown are the children and grandchildren of Brown parents. Many, if not a majority of Brown parents do not see the school primarily as fitting their children to earn a living. They want it to be a pleasant environment which promotes the intellectual, cultural and emotional development of their children.

In 1970, the parents at Brown became aware that Brown was at the top of Metro Obsolescence Survey, which meant that in terms of quite a few criteria, it was the most obsolete school in Metro. They began to enquire into the possibility of renovating, but found it would cost almost as much as putting up a new building.

Long before a new school was thought of, they had been renting facilities all over the Brown School area for an extremely well-organized and well-financed after-school program which offered the children a wide range of sports, crafts and cultural activities. Since they were already aware of the deficiencies of the old school, they started thinking of the new school and what they wanted it to be.

One of the parents on the building committee is an architect, and he was able to give them some expert counsel. They had many meetings among themselves, with their trustees, with Board officials, with different school officials in other boroughs. They came to the conclusion that they had to have a new building and they wanted to make sure that the Toronto Board and the Metro Board went to the Province for approval and that replacement funds for Brown were included in the Capital Program.

They prepared an excellent, technically very professional slide presentation, with a synchronized sound track. Nothing like it had ever been presented to the Board. The slide show of the facilities and programs at Brown and at other schools made the point very vividly. The Board was impressed. Brown School was duly approved for replacement and the architect parent on the building committee was appointed to draw up the plans.

At this time, one of the parents who is President of the Association of Women Electors of Toronto and who had been an observer at City Parks and Recreation for years, came forward with the information that City Parks and Recreation had over $1 million put aside in its budget for a Recreation Centre in North Toronto. After some preliminary discussions, it was found that the city is forbidden by provincial legislation from cooperating with other public bodies on the building of anything but swimming pools if it does not own the property. For the city to incorporate community recreational facilities into Brown School, the legislation would have to be changed. The Brown parents lobbied their MPP's, the Board, and City and Metro councils. The legislation was changed in June, 1972. The plans for the school had by now reached an advanced stage. The architect had drawn up the plans, the city would be cooperating to the tune of about $442,000.00, the second and third phase of submissions and approvals had all gone through City Parks and Recreation, the Toronto and Metro Committees and Board and on to the province, when a serious impediment developed. People to the south objected to the proposed location of the school on the western end of the property because it would interfere with their view. They were determined to take their case through the Committee of Adjustment and the Ontario Municipal Board. This threatened to delay the plans for as long as three years. It had originally been planned to use the old building while the new school was under construction, but now, to avoid the delay, the community decided to have the old school torn down. The children would be housed in portables for a full year while the new school was being built on the site of the old.

At a time when school as we know it is rapidly changing, Brown School has set a large number of precedents. The Brown community will have unparalleled access to community facilities and an immersion French stream will start in Kindergarten in the fall of 1972. Its new building, to be completed by the fall of 1973, will be flexible enough to accommodate these and many more functions now and in the future. All this has been accomplished by parents and non-parent residents whose level of aspiration and achievement is among the highest of any community anywhere, working on all levels of government through every conceivable channel.

Park School and Oak St. School

If the Brown area can be called a community of advantage, then certainly Regent Park is a community of disadvantage.

Almost all the children in Park School live in Regent Park, a huge, grim public housing project consisting of identical four-story brick buildings situated in the midst of a bleak Cabbagetown ghetto. It has no recreational or social amenities, no trees, no gardens, so little lawn that what there is has been scraped up by thousands of children's feet to be replaced by concrete. But the area does provide low-cost housing, a scarce commodity in the inner city. For 3,000 adults and 6,000 youngsters no other choice is open.

Several years ago, the Toronto Board, intending to relieve the pressure on several of the schools around Regent Park, expropriated 55 houses in one block on Oak Street. In its wisdom it saw no need to consult with the residents about the proposed site. The community attempted to resist the destruction of their homes and the building of a school in what they deemed an undesirable location. Many meetings were held and representations made but to no avail. All the families, the hold-outs, the last sick old couple, all were eventually dislodged and except for one house, the block was razed.

No school has as yet been built at Oak Street. It is now a vacant lot. When it is built, it will be what the community has decided it needs. Groups of parents have complained loudly that their children cannot read and as a result are being shunted off into dead-end vocational schools and "opportunity" classes. They have been called "an ill-trained Greek chorus" by one witty trustee, in an "amusing" aside and genetically inferior by another. The effects of a foul environment, unemployment, illness, bad housing, poor nutrition and pre-natal care are, of course, not considered by those who excuse social evils by blaming the victims. It is my hope that, whatever the final decision about Oak Street School, it will bring something of gardens and shrubs and variety and colour into a landscape of drabness and monotony.

Though the neighbourhood may lack charm, it is not lacking in community spirit. This is apparent in several new educational programs available to the residents of Regent

Park. Since the mothers of Regent Park in their "ill-trained" way started trying to do things for their disadvantaged community, the Board has become much more approachable. In 1970, to inquire into the mothers' grievances, it ran the most comprehensive demographic survey ever undertaken, of all 110,000 children in the Toronto school system. Known as the Every Student Survey, it found, not surprisingly, that the results bore out what the mothers had been saying all along. Now that the officials had their hard data, their correlations between economic, ethnic and educational patterns from the Board computer, they had no hesitaton in recommending that an Inner City Task Force be set up. Its job would be to assist citizen groups anywhere in the city who wanted to initiate community projects. The Task Force (consisting of a former inspector and a former teacher-turned-social worker-turned-community organizer with back-up research and secretarial help) operating from Oak Street House, the one house still left standing.

In the past two years, many of the concerns and discontents of the Park parents have been uncovered. An Early Childhood Program uses a portable provided by the Board. It was started by the mothers, and is run entirely by them. Children from two months on are enrolled. The ratio is almost one to one, because the parents cannot bring their children into the program unless they themselves work in it. A teacher comes in from George Brown College to conduct seminars, show films, and so on. Some of the women are enrolled in the Psychology course at Ryerson Open College, which has no prerequisites. The community has set up young peoples' programs and a Summer Day Camp on a country property on loan from a private benefactor. Many parents are now working with the teachers in the school, assisting in the reading program both at home and at school. Sound and reasonable recommendations have been sent to the Board in brief after brief. Slowly, one by one, they are being adopted and implemented.

Though Park School is of exactly the same vintage as

Brown, there are no plans to replace it at the moment. Whatever the reasons the fact is that the controversies surrounding Park School have not focused on the need for a new building. The people here are primarily interested in programs which will give their children some semblance of equal educational opportunity. More than a building, these people evidently needed the opportunity to voice their legitimate concerns. The articulation of these concerns gave a very real focus to their efforts to give their children a better chance. In the process, they are learning to identify their problems and to find the collective and personal remedies. It is this active process of renewal which has characterized the efforts of the Regent Park parents, no less than the parents of Brown. The common cause which will yield the elusive energizer known as Equality of Opportunity may well lie in such self-activation of ghetto communities.

Kensington

One of the first communities to take the community school route was Kensington, formerly known as the Jewish Market. The residents, now predominantly Portuguese, maintain an Old World neighbourhood in the midst of the central core. As such, it is in itself a kind of school in which newcomers from the towns and villages of Europe learn the ways of the New World.

Kensington became conscious of its identity as a life support to European immigrants during a fight against expropriation by hungry "developers" and a destructive urban renewal plan. Later the threat posed by the Spadina Expressway maintained and strengthened the feeling of common purpose. So when the School Board, aware of the alarming overcrowding at Ryerson School, decided to build a junior school in the Kensington area, the community was ready.

Out of the consultations (which never became confrontations) came a pleasing and imaginative design for the new school which has bonded the school to the community before even opening its doors. But the door at 110 Oxford Street is seldom closed. 110 Oxford Street is a house used by the principal who has been working in the area for over a year. The residents flow through the doors at all hours and for all possible reasons. Clubs, advice, social activities, language classes, all this and more goes on every day. Kensington School promises to be a happy, busy place and there is little doubt that the community will be well served.

Kingsley

An efficient and humane delivery system was needed for a multitude of social services to the residents of Pelham Park, a huge, public housing complex and its neighbourhood in west-central Toronto. This led the community to focus on the new junior school planned for the district. Many committees, many meetings later, the Board was asked to approve the plans and the name "Kingsley Community Resource Centre". The plans, attractive, imaginative and flexible, were approved, but legislative constraints led the Board back to the designation "school". As a result, the new building, which will have the facilities and services of many agencies within its walls, will be called the Kingsley Community School. But when it opens in the fall of 1973, with its services easily accessible to all, everyone will know it for what it really is – a resource for the whole community.

Balmy Beach

The east end of Toronto or "Beaches" area is noteworthy for several things. It is WASP, very "Orange" and predominantly working-class. Balmy Beach School, a very old school, is about to be replaced. One of the trustees in the area has tried for years to establish a "traditional school". There flourishes in the area an organization known as C.A.M.P.S. – the Committee Against Moral Pollution in the Schools. Another group called the Parents Action League, opposed to "progressive education" and advocating a return to fundamental skills and no frills, has many members in the area.

Many parents want their children home for lunch and see the senior school (Grades 7 and 8) as a threat to close family life because the lunch period is only 40 minutes long.

Put all these opinions together, circulate a petition asking for a Kindergarten to Grade 8 (K-8) school which will teach the Christian virtues that collects over one thousand signatures and then try to decide what kind of school the community needs. Should it be Kindergarten to Grade 6 open plan; K-6 egg-crate, fundamental skills; K-8 ungraded; K-8 Christian virtues (long lunch)?

The Board approved a K-6 school, then heard about the petition asking for K-8. The Board asked Metro to revise the approval to allow for K-8. Another group petitioned the Board saying that the previous petition had been signed by many non-residents. At this writing, the Board has approved a K-6 school but the plans must allow for a possible addition for Grades 7 and 8. The architect is spending a great deal of time meeting with groups in the area about the school design. A demographer is to survey the whole district. A planned addition to Glen Ames Senior School is to be held in abeyance until the issue at Balmy Beach is resolved. It may take a while.

Laneway

Cabbagetown is the most economically depressed area in Toronto. It contains street after street of human problems. Many of the chronic welfare families exist here, barely making it from cheque to cheque. How pride or hope or dignity have ever managed to survive in these degrading conditions is hard to imagine. Yet among a few of the residents of this area there arose a feeling that it could not be entirely their fault that their children did so badly in school. Why did so many drop out? Why could so few read well? Could it be the school, the teaching methods, the class size? Was opportunity class good for the children? There seemed to be no answer within the system.

However, several mothers felt that what was offered to their children was not enough. They opened their own school – Laneway. Free quarters in Dixon Hall for two young teachers (paid by the Students' Administrative Council at the University of Toronto) and ten children withdrawn from opportunity classes and vocational school provided them with the chance to try it their way for two years. Reading skills developed dramatically along with self-esteem. But in June 1972 the money for the teachers ceased. The Board, interested in what has developed, has, at the request of Laneway, taken the fledgling under its wing and will operate it as a public school starting in the fall of 1972. The governance of the school will remain as much in the hands of its present group as is possible. Whether it survives or not remains to be seen.

Alpha

The Hall-Dennis report is alive and well! A group of Toronto parents who would like to see an elementary school run on purely Hall-Dennis lines have met weekly among themselves for months. They presented their ideas to the Board for approval, have found a building to rent, have interviewed and recommended for hiring the teachers and are set to open in the fall of 1972 if the Ontario Fire Marshal approves their building. One hundred children are ready to participate with their parents in ALPHA (A Lot of People Hoping for an Alternative). They range from three and a half years old on up to high school age. Instead of the usual neighbourhood type of school, this one will draw from the entire city and will use the whole Metropolitan area as its campus. The school will be governed democratically. Staff, students, parents, trustees, all will have their say. The Board approved group met with the Board's "Alternatives Committee" many times to iron out details and procedures .Although many of the prime movers in ALPHA are academics and professional people, they want the school to be a cross-section of society. It will be interesting to see if they succeed.

Contact

In the spring of 1972, a group of concerned vocational

school teachers approached the Board's Alternatives Committee with a proposal. They wanted the Board to allow four of their number to recruit fifty drop-outs or potential dropouts from the city schools and work out a "reclamation project" called "Contact". The teachers felt that many of the students dropping out, from the vocational schools especially, did so because of poor reading and lack of other fundamental skills. In a clearly structured setting with individually designed programs, the teachers felt that they could restore the self-esteem of these students and thereby improve their academic ability. The Board was very interested in the Contact idea and it is hoped that the school will open in January 1973. The Regent Park area has shown great enthusiasm for Contact and would like to have it based there. A worker for the YMCA attached to the Regent Park area told the Board, when a trustee wondered if fifty students could be found, that he could find four hundred in Regent Park alone! What is interesting about Contact is that it is teacher-initiated. Is this a community?

Seed

In the spring of 1968, a group of concerned elementary school teachers developed a plan for a volunteer information service to students who wanted something useful to do in their summer holidays. The Board gave them a room, some telephones and printed hundreds of posters. Any student who wanted to learn Spanish, discuss politics, make a radio program, play the guitar better, or any one of dozens of choices could phone the number on the poster. He would be told where the group he wanted was meeting. A new group would start whenever several similar requests had been received. Adult volunteers came forward in droves. Very little money was spent but hundreds of students and dozens of community volunteers worked together all summer. SEED, meaning "A Summer of Experience, Exploration and Discovery", was an overnight success.

Many of the same volunteers and students started up again

in the summer of 1969. This time however, eighteen of the groups involving close to ninety students, kept their classes going all winter in churches, offices and homes. The total cost for the winter program was 35 cents for a duplicate key to the church that served as an office.

A new Board took office in January 1970. They had barely settled in when the SEED students presented a brief requesting a full-time, ungraded, accredited secondary school for 100 pupils. It would need a staff of five and would utilize the network of volunteers as in the summer program. Students would be chosen by lot. Premises would be needed in a central location so that the students could have easy access to the university and all the other midtown institutions that they used.

The Alternatives Committee of the Board wrestled with the SEED proposal for several months. One by one, obstacles were overcome and on September 15, 1970, the lottery was held. SEED will start its third full year of operation this fall with 120 students. The Board rents several rooms and a basement office from the YMHA at the corner of Bloor and Spadina. It is one block from U. of T., half a block from a subway station and across the street from the College of Education.

At SEED the community is, in theory, all the staff, all the parents, all the students and all the volunteers. Working this out in practical terms, however, has not been easy. But this spring, when a new coordinator and two new teachers were needed, a sensible and amicable procedure was proposed, approved by the Board and implemented. The entire staff, several students, three parents, a representative of the Director of Education and a trustee constituted the selection committee. They interviewed all the qualified applicants, discussed the choices carefully, voted by secret ballot and forwarded their slate to the Director for his approval. The Board ratified these choices in July.

The new coordinator of SEED taught at the school in 1970-71. His daughter is a student there. He can therefore approach the "community" problem from several angles. In a school without compulsory attendance, grades or even classes, the problems are, of course, unique. SEED requires a high degree of self-motivation, self-discipline and responsibility to the group from its participants for survival. The students tend to be bright, articulate and rather anarchistic. Their resistance to "structure" makes cooperative action and decision-making difficult. Leadership under these constraints, has to be of a very high, and tactful, order. But the results promise to be worth the effort.

* * *

In the preceding instances of community involvement in Toronto schools, what was done, and the way it was done, differ markedly. It is patently impossible to generalize from individual instances on the basis of any assumed characteristics of some "ideal type" of community school. However, this sample does document some of the circumstances which prompt people to take action resulting in something which can be called "a community school".

While most of the action was taken by people living in an actual geographical community already served by a conventional school, some was taken by people with a common purpose, as in Laneway, SEED, and Contact. In some cases action was taken because schools were on the "Obsolescence List" (i.e., slated for replacement), in others because the residents felt the community was not being served well or at all. It is perhaps noteworthy that the one factor common to all is that in one way or another, the people involved all felt themselves threatened by impersonal forces which do not recognize them either as individuals or as communities.

The vice-principal of one of our inner-city high schools in his farewell speech at the final staff luncheon, commented somewhat sarcastically, "Compulsion is out, community is in." In view of the fact that this prediction was offered along with his figures on the total number of absentee sheets which had been processed that year as well as the total number of new pupils who would be eagerly flocking to the school next year, it is unlikely that he was expecting any immediate impact of the community concept on the secondary schools. No doubt he would subscribe to the Cubs and Brownies view of the community use of schools. Because the changes likely to result from this minimal view will at best be no more than an additional irritant, it is crucial to work out a proper definition of a community school.

The power base for public schools is not in compulsory attendance, but in parents' faith in the future. Many parents have lost faith in the system, but they cannot, they dare not, lose faith in a future for their children. The schools, moribund bureaucracies though they may be, persist, not so much because they babysit, or keep the young from entering the labour force, but because, in their own distorted and amorphous way, they represent the hopes that parents have for their children.

The parents and other community-minded groups who have figured in creating these new community schools in Toronto have returned to that original source of power. They know that schools represent society's contribution to a future for their children. They know that, somewhere in the shuffle, the goals of public education have been lost. They have learned that society is themselves, acting in association with others to whom they are linked by the same overriding necessity. And they are committed not only to ensuring the future of their children, but that there will be a future at all. There is no doubt that they have shown the way to a highly productive interaction between local, municipal and provincial administrative levels in the creation of these community schools.

1   Position Paper, *New Dimensions*, Ministry of Education of Ontario, April 1972.

The Limits of Community Schools

D. A. MacIver

The expression "community school" may mean anything from a school managed by experts in order to respond to what they perceive as the needs of the community, to a school" is mentioned without any qualification it is the kind paper the definition that will be adopted is one that lies between the extremes suggested, i.e. a community school is a school supported by public funds and managed so that it responds to the needs of the students attending the school. The people who manage the school will be parents, teachers, administrators, and, depending on the circumstances, may include students and other citizens. When "community school" is mentioned without any qualification it is the kind of institution defined in the last two sentences that is referred to.

The community school idea is rapidly developing into the latest educational fad. This is a pity because fads come and go and when they have gone all that remains is an empty promise. There is no doubt that the community school idea has much to offer contemporay education but the concept needs to be considered critically. The major problem with the community school concept seems to be that it is perceived as being generally applicable whereas in fact its present area of application is probably quite small. If the community school works well in certain limited areas, it may be developed elsewhere, but it is more likely that schools managed by specialists will remain the norm.

An important truism is that different communities have different life styles. These differences, if the arguments of progressives are accepted, should have an influence on the kind of school that serves any given community. The dominant influence on any community is the nature of the employment of the adult residents. Thus, in a community of lawyers, doctors, dentists, business men, air line pilots, and so on, no less than in a community of mechanics, truckers, carpenters, steelworkers, and technicians, the life style is influenced by the rigours of working hours and by the orientation of specialism. But not only are the males controlled by the clock and the world view of a specialist. Wives too pursue independent careers or else organize their lives around the careers of their husbands and children. In other words, most people are specialists and live according to tightly organized schedules.

In such "communities of specialists" schools are important. They operate according to the sort of clock time that is followed by adults. Most parents believe that when they send their children to school they will be well looked after. This has been denigrated as "baby sitting", but many would argue that it is this act of care which enables both parents to pursue their careers or to fulfil themselves in other directions. Besides being cared for, children learn the basic academic skills; are "disciplined" to accept the dominant norms of their society; and are introduced to leisure activities.

The school as described is no mere convenience, but an integral feature of contemporary society. It is perceived by parents as an institution run by specialists for the complementary good of other specialists and for the benefit of their children. In the terms that parents use to assess schools, these institutions have been quite effective. Because of the effectiveness of traditional schools there appears to most people to be no good reason for changing the way they are managed, and parents are, in fact, showing no great enthusiasm to participate in the schools at the "management" level. This is not to deny that some parents do involve themselves in the activities of the schools. A small percentage who have free time contribute to the school as part of their own organized activities. But generally these tasks are of a pretty mundane nature: listening to children read; driving cars for school trips; acting as chaperones; serving as library assistants and so on. Even when the parents' activities are more sophisticated (teaching weaving, pottery, or contributing in other specialized areas of work) it is quite clear that most parents see themselves as simply aiding the teacher, who is the expert, in the work of teaching.

Thus, the schools of specialists, which are typified in suburban areas, seem to serve a particular group of people in satisfactory ways. Parents accept this service as part of their life style and they accept it as morally sound. Even in the most staid communities of specialists, of course, there will be dissidents, and teachers and principals may sometimes be amongst them. These are the people who have to sell the concept of community schools to the community at large but they have a tough job before them. Their task is basically one of interfering with a life style by inducing people to withdraw from some of the activities they now perform, to move from their self-chosen paths and, instead, to learn about school management, to spend time in classrooms, to develop curriculum and so on. The difficulty is accentuated by the fact that most people see no reason to interfere with the specialists who already do these things.

In most areas when an effort is made to establish community school councils the response is usually quite small. Exceptions occur in communities that have some particular reason for establishing such councils and where dedicated individuals use sophisticated techniques to persuade others to join them. Nevertheless the establishment of such school councils may be inconsistent with the general ethos of the communty. Other people in the community, perhaps a majority, may prefer to let schools be run by specialists. That is, communities of specialists identify more closely with the specialists who run the schools (and who are also members of the community) than with those atypical individuals in the community who desire to interfere with the work of specialists. And all this is perfectly understandable because the typical school is seen by so many people to have served a useful function, while it lets them get on with earning a living or fulfilling themselves in other ways.

But the success of schools supported by public taxation is by no means universal. In particular, inner-city and immigrant areas do not appear to have been well served. There are many reasons for this, including the fact that such communities are not usually communities of specialists. This may be explained by stating that the typical school run by specialists and oriented to a middle-class life style has not responded adequately to other communities that perceive specialists and middle-class values as foreign encroachments. In communities where unemployment is rife, welfare is common, single parent families occur with greater frequency than usual, and where chronic illness is a greater possibility than elsewhere in society, the value system of the traditional school simply does not make much sense to the residents.

In such situations an alien institution, the school, is implanted into a community. As long as that school is simply run by specialists, it is likely to remain alien. In these cases parents, teachers, and student must confront each other, discuss, argue and seek solutions which make sense to the child. The real community school of parents, teachers, and students working together to capitalize on the knowledge, attitudes, and values of the inner city seems to be an essential first step in making education more equal. If there really are fewer people regularly employed in the inner city, then it is possible that more parents will be available to deal with the time consuming matter of school management and curriculum development. Besides hammering out suitable programs the meetings of teachers and parents will permit mutual learning about each other to take place. This learning will be enhanced if parents also participate in the teaching of the program that they help to devise. The mere presence of an aware parent in a room may give her a greater understanding of her child and may have the additional benefit that she may pick up something which had been lost in her own education. But the learning is reciprocal and the teacher can benefit much from an inner-city parent who is concerned about the future of her children. Clearly, in such situations as these a community school, of the kind defined, would be perfectly appropriate.

To this point an attempt has been made to show that the community school concept is useful in some situations but not in all. But there are more generic problems with the community school issue that need to be considered. For example, for some years now students have been given an ever widening choice in the selection of the school programs. Something may happen to that choice when, and if, community schools become the norm. That is, sophisticated people with dogmatic religious or political beliefs may run schools like tight ships and with the full support of parents, so that few complaints are likely to be heard if students are mistreated. On the other hand, some schools may be run loosely with virtually no control over the students and with no effort to introduce any particular political or religious beliefs. In fact, they will be "run" anarchically. While parents and students have rights which they may exercise there are definite limits to those rights. The extent to which a state can permit education to be diversified is not yet known. Is it possible, for example, for people who have been educated in quite different fashions to live together harmoniously? These are questions that tend to be ignored because they are not immediate, but it is essential that anyone interested in Canada consider to what extent the present general "good order" of society is dependent upon the fact that virtually everyone went to the same kind of school. Individualism is an essential quality of a democratic society, but so is a common core of values. Autonomous community schools will ensure the former but not necessarily the latter.

Associated with the possibility of education becoming

highly diversified and strongly influenced by lay people, is the fact that individual schools will develop highly distinctive modes of operation.Some observers believe that education is about to experience important technical developments which will have to be managed by those who are properly trained. It is true that at the moment the more successful community school efforts seem to be spearheaded by university academics, who would obviously be in a position to handle these kinds of techniques. But there are limits to the numbers of professors who can perform this kind of missionary work and sophisticated approaches may be reduced to a simple and misleading level in the hands of untrained people. A current example of the tendency to propose simplistic answers to the problems of teaching students to read is apparent in the view of certain groups concerned with inner-city education. They believe that all that is needed is greater control and better order and then children will come to learn to read. Even at the moment there is enough research to indicate that this will not do. The problems of inner-city education are much more complex than this. Once the teacher has become familiar with the inner-city life style, he may then "know" how to do things, and the whole business of lay-teacher meetings may become an empty charade.

This stage is not yet with us and it has already been argued that for inner-city situations the community school seems to be an essential first step. Like all ideas in education, however, the community school concept has to be treated with caution and judgement. It does not appear to be the best approach in all areas of society at the moment. In those areas of society where it does appear to be the best approach conditions may demand radical change in that approach as time goes on. There are latent problems of parochialism inherent in the idea of community schools and these may have an adverse "influence" on Canadian society in general. Finally, it will be ironic if the specialists eventually do come through with effective ways of learning and teaching, and if a lay public inhibits the development of those techniques in the areas where their effectiveness will be most useful.

Community College Development in Saskatchewan: A Unique Approach

Ron Faris

Saskatchewan is at it again. John Diefenbaker's "fellow Canadians" are duly warned that once again novel social inventions will be coming out of the West. Perhaps one of the most exciting and important will be the development of a unique form of community college.

The development of community colleges for Saskatchewan has been discussed for almost a decade. In fact the college saga appears to have had more installments than the "Whiteoaks of Jalna". For instance, a commission chaired by Dr. J. W. Spink, President of the University of Saskatchewan, recommended in 1967 that a college system be created to provide "middle range education". In 1970 an advisory committee report to the then Education Minister urged that a system of "colleges of applied arts and sciences" be initiated in the province's four largest cities, based upon the already existing technical and vocational facilities. The report also included a draft of college legislation.

With the advent of a provincial election in the spring of 1971 it appeared that college development might become an issue. At a Young Liberal rally the late Premier Thatcher raised colleges as an election issue. He also intimated that a college system's major role would be the provision of the first two years of university – essentially a junior college model. The NDP avoided a direct confrontation on the issue but did emphasize an alleged lack of Liberal leadership in educational matters. The NDP "New Deal" program did, however, promise the establishment of "regional education centres to bring educational opportunities closer to the people of Saskatchewan." It also promised to expand opportunities for educational upgrading and retraining for adults. In the main, the non-debate on community colleges left any voters who cared with a choice between confusion and vagueness.

With the election of an NDP government the Honourable Gordon MacMurchy, Minister of Education, called two invitational conferences to discuss the development of colleges in the province. The first meeting, held on October 8, 1971, was primarily to assess the existing draft legislation. The consensus of that meeting was that the proposed legislation was too narrow in scope, emphasizing essentially academic and technical-vocational development but expressing virtually no concern for the growth of community education and development. There was general agreement that Saskatchewan must develop a unique community college system with emphasis on community education and development. The existing legislation was, therefore, laid aside.

At the second conference on December 1, 1971, participants emphasized that community-oriented colleges could be developed only if the assistance and commitment of people in local communities was gained. Further, it was urged that rural education be a major concern of the community college system. It was also emphasized that, in order to develop a truly community-oriented system, the process of community education and development must be initiated at the formative stages so that local people could have a major role in deciding what sort of colleges developed in their region.

Following the December conference, Mr. MacMurchy appointed an advisory committee composed of individuals with a wide range of experience in a variety of Saskatchewan's continuing education programs. The committee's task was to advise on the processes of community education and development necessary for the growth of community-oriented colleges. It held fifty public meetings in southern and central portions of the province and six in the North. Thus from Uranium City in the North to Coronach in the South, Lloydminster in the West to Moosomin in the East, thousands of citizens became involved in discussing what a community college would mean to them and their community. The format of the meetings was simple – a brief presentation of the college concept by a committee member, clarifying questions and comments, followed by group discussions of how a relevant college could serve the local community. The Committee also received letters and briefs from interested citizens and organizations. Seven principles, stressing the community involvement and service aspects of the development had been enunciated by the Department of Education and were used as the basis of discussion. Though a wide range of interpretation of and response to these principles was stimulated, the ultimate effect of these meetings was to establish a consensus which permitted the definition of a practical acceptable working model.

The concept is essentially of a community college in which the community is the campus. The "college" will exist wherever its programs are offered. There is no intention of creating a building campaign nor of constructing either mini-universities (junior colleges) or small-scale technical institutes. Indeed, the college will be chiefly a coordinating and facilitating agency rather than a programming instituion. The existing learning resources of a variety of government and voluntary agencies will be used whenever possible.

Colleges will, however, fill educational gaps. College community education workers, operating out of store front locations in a satellite organization structure, will assist in identifying local and regional needs and assessing available programs. They will also assist in matching needs with local resources, physical and human, wherever feasible. Only when local resources are non-existent or insufficient will wider, provincial resources such as those of the university or the technical institutes be used.

Unique inter-agency relations will, it is hoped, be developed. The provincial library system, with over 250 branches, will serve as a college library-media distribution system. The University of Saskatchewan will provide its programs, possibly on a contractual basis, upon request from local college councils as will the three provincial technical-vocational institutes.

The province-wide meetings clarified many other matters. For instance, a strong sense of community still exists in much of rural Saskatchewan. It is also evident that a wide range of learning opportunities is desired and that many untapped resources exist in Saskatchewan. Expert farmers, local artists and teachers, all with knowledge or skills worth sharing can become part of the instructional and community education staff of their college.

As a result of the meetings the committee became even more aware of the unique nature of every community they visited and of the necessity to develop a college system flexible enough to meet varying community needs and aspirations. The committee also became aware of the differing responses to the college concept. While it was generally well received by those who participated in the meetings it became clear that in most cases the smaller the community the greater the support.

Education Minister MacMurchy has already publicly stated his intention of giving priority to rural college development. He has also encouraged the use of local farmers as part of the community education and development staff in that six month period between harvest and seeding. It is the hope of the advisory committee that the initial emphasis on community education and development, the use of local people in its process, and the creation of small administrative and professional units in the college system will reduce, if not prevent, early organizational institutionalization and ossification.

One belief shared by many Saskatchewanians is that the province has often led Canada in the creation of more humane ways of meeting human needs. The Community

College Advisory Committee feels that they are looking at potentially the most exciting community college system in Canada. No other system has the commitment to community education and development which this will have. No other system in Canada will be as committed to serving the needs of rural people as this system. The advisory committee is urging the adoption of exciting models and principles in the development of the Saskatchewan community college system. If community colleges cannot be truly community-oriented in Saskatchewan, they probably cannot be community-oriented in Canada.

The Big Blue Schoolhouse: The Davis Era in Ontario Education

Walter Pitman

As the decade of the Sixties was coming to an end, Claire Westcott, executive asistant to the Minister of Education, suggested that in view of the fact that such an incomparable expansion of activity had taken place in the recent past, someone should be assigned to chronicle these events. It is to the credit of the Minister, William Davis that he realized an "official history" would be inappropriate. Yet someone had to be found who was familiar with the Ontario educational scene, who had connections with those in the far-flung empire of "the department" and who had the research and writing skills to produce a readable piece of work. The person selected was Dr. W. Gerald Fleming, who had been central to the creation of the Ontario Institute for Studies in Education and who had participated in a wide range of activities associated with the educational enterprise throughout the province. The result was the eight-volume series entitled *Ontario's Educative Society*.

One stands in awe of the magnitude of the work. That any man, with some research help admittedly, could have within a couple of years produced the several thick volumes which make up this series leaves one breathless with awe. Yet the work is exhaustively researched, and is based on the most contemporary sources. As well it is imaginatively organized and interestingly written. In short, it is a major addition to the social history of this province and no one who purports to know something about Ontario's educational system will be able to avoid reading this extensive chronicle of the major events of the "Davis Years".

It is not, however, a searching, philosophical analysis of the learning process in the Ontario jurisdiction. Even less is it a complete historical record – for though there is proper recognition that most of our institutions are firmly rooted in a century of development, these references are usually brief and introductory in character. It is obvious that Fleming's concern is with the contemporary scene, and how the policies of the Sixties will influence the future.

One canot help but be concerned by the title, *Ontario's Educative Society*, for essentially these volumes are about Ontario's Schooling Process. That, perhaps, is the triumph and the tragedy of the Sixties. We have made monumental efforts to reform and humanize our schools, colleges and universities only to find that the solution to the shaping of a learning community lies not in institutionalizing and isolating the learner – but encouraging a commitment to emotional and intellectual development throughout the society. One reads this massive opus with a sad heart – perhaps nothing but the decline and fall of these institutions can clear the way for a dynamic and vital explosion of creativity encompassing the entire citizenry. In fairness to the author, the dichotomy between education and schooling is touched upon in the introduction and it may well be a theme of the companion volume to the series, *Education; Ontario's Preoccupation,* a work which will provide Fleming greater opportunity for the expression of more unorthodox and imaginative views on his subject.

The most pointed criticism of these volumes will come from those who have seen the Davis years as a period of conservative revolution, of change without direction, of explosive expansion without counting the cost, of unparalleled activity without any concept of priority. For these critics, Fleming's blandness and unemotional descriptive narrative will be a blasphemy. For indeed, it is a bloodless business. There is no high drama, no emotional confrontation but rather a logical, pragmatic development of necessary programs and institutions to meet the obvious needs of a technological society. Throughout the account there seems to be an unstated assumption that Ontario has the best educational system in the world, and that even with Fleming's occasional misgivings, it is about as good as can be expected. One can almost hear the slogan "Is there any place you'd rather be?".

How unfortunate for these observers that a few more months had not transpired before the publication of *Ontario's Educative Society* – for with ceilings on expenditure some of the new programs spawned by the expansiveness of the Davis administration are threatened. There are thousands of certified teachers without jobs and the morale of those with jobs has never been lower. The university community is united in a way never before experienced – united in their despair over the Draft Report on Post-Secondary Education. It could be said that Bill Davis left the helm at just the right moment politically – and the timing of Fleming's work could not have been more propitious for a positive record of achievement virtually without blemish.

Another author must take up the task of seeing the activities of the Davis decade from the perspective of the Seventies, not as an exercise in critical hindsight and not merely as an inevitable response to a world suddenly and mindlessly obsessed with education as the solution to every problem. Now the questions are arising. The Davis years were characterized by an exciting explosion of experiments and innovation. The contrast to the Dunlop years is one which Fleming draws without restraint, and he spares no venom in his assessment of that Minister's inadequacies. However, even the clarity of Fleming's presentation does not hide the "ad hockery", the lack of planning associated with specific goals and uncoordinated with any total response – surely the major criticism of William G. Davis as Minister.

Many examples come to mind. Educational television has developed at great expense and the programs which were produced gained world-wide recognition and acclaim. But where can one find any clear, concise statement of the role of television, either in the formal schooling process or as an informal aspect of child development? Where does one find any philosophy of educational technology which might have been a guide to teachers and trustees in sorting out their priorities, to say nothing of the chaos and expense resulting from the purchase of uncoordinated technical equipment? This lack of intellectual awareness about the nature of a new teaching device and the simplistic response that it was "an extension of the text-book," when one of the world's most imaginative theorists on understanding media and their messages was a stone's throw from the Minister's office, is staggering.

Although the Davis years courageously attacked the problem of the proliferation of small, incompetent school boards and created the county board system, there was no effective change in the direction of providing structures for greater parental and teacher involvement – and alienation and disaffection resulted, not a happy basis on which to build the system of the Seventies when ceilings, accountability and rationalization have become the key words. Even more surprising, the belief that the administrative revolution could be accomplished without a basic revision of the financial support system exacerbated the already developing outrage at the costs of education and those who work in schools and colleges will pay the price of that short-sightedness. Nor was there any dynamic, interactive relationship between the Department and the new boards, which might have spawned a more positive, creative method of determining goals and priorities than the mere imposition of ceilings by the Department followed upon by the angry, confrontational reactions of trustees.

*　　*　　*

The *Hall-Dennis Report,* a document which some will call Davis's crowning achievement – and others will characterize as the record of his bankruptcy – is given considerable attention in these volumes. And the document has had a real effect on the schooling of our children in Ontario. But the real tragedy was that, instead of using the interest and excitement created by the Report, as an opportunity to explore new education structures and new relationships between administrators, teachers, trustees and parents, the document became the battleground for the debating of conservative and liberal views on education. Never was there a profound, serious, high priority effort to look critically at the curriculum – at what we are doing day by day in the classroom in a decade of unprecedented change. Nor was any effort made to look at the rôle of the teacher, at a time when the careers of other professionals were under close scrutiny. Nor were any structures created for bringing into effect those recommendations which would have improved the system.

Perhaps Davis will be remembered most warmly for the development of the Colleges of Applied Arts and Technology. Yet, even the greatest achievement had flaws which came as a result of this pervading lack of careful consideration. The Colleges are perhaps the most imaginative, uninhibited and least tradition-bound institutions – but how unfortunate that more opportunities for participation and decision sharing have not been the hallmark of these institutions. Indeed, they stand outside the mainstream of intellectual freedom with their faculties in some half-way house between the status of public servants and professionals. Nor does Fleming exhibit any strong appreciation of the irresponsibility of providing training for hundreds of young people, in these institutions, only to find that provincial government departments, or supported agencies refuse to accept their qualifications for certain specific jobs.

Perhaps the most obvious example of the lack of priority during the Davis years is the state of teacher education. While every speaker mouthed the litany that the most important aspect of the educational process was the quality and commitment of the teacher in the classroom, in reality teacher education received the least attention and financial support of all the various functions of the Department of Education.

It is easy to say that the McLeod Report and the subsequent acceptance of its recommendations by the Minister, placed this process in a state of transition from teachers' colleges to the campuses of the province's universities. But the fact that the simplistic notion that the problems of adequate teacher education would inevitably be solved by the physical move to the university setting was deemed logical indicates the limitations of leadership in the Davis years. How incredible that, with the burgeoning complexity of teaching in a technological society, there was no provincial priority given to the preparation of teachers, and that our classrooms are still inhabited by so many threatened, unsure, unimaginative teachers who have neither the skills to build a curriculum for their students and who are so nervous of sharing decisions and responsibilities with parents, students and other teachers.

Amidst this affluence, there are examples of neglect, a neglect reflected in Fleming's emphasis. If our concern about the unfortunate (such as the trainable retarded) is the most effective method of judging our system, then the mere five lines and a statistical chart in Volume 1 with a few pages in his account, is a splendid articulation of our comparative neglect of so many of those in need. For along with the retarded, we have little to be proud of in our efforts on behalf of the emotionally disturbed, the culturally and economically deprived, to say nothing of our treatment of the children of our native peoples and immigrants. Fleming recognizes the problems but nothing of the agony of the children and their parents – only a comparative silence which will some day be broken by a very different study of Ontario's educational system.

In some of Fleming's pages one gains a glimpse of the future – a phrase or a line, but never a full-blown picture, for he is concerned with appreciative analysis of past decisions, not prophecy. So one reads volume after volume wishing that a man who had such a vast grasp of the Sixties could have charted the direction of the contrasting Seventies.

Although financial restraints have dominated the thinking of all connected with education so far, this subject will be displaced by a hard-nosed reversal of priorities in many areas. It scarcely takes an expert to perceive certain trends.

Early childhood education will receive the dominant attention and it will not be merely a matter of bringing children into school at an earlier age but will also emphasize an outreach into the home and family, a process which will bring parents into the school not only as volunteer assistants but as participants in the decisions about the curriculum and the rules of procedure. For this is the kernel of reality about the community school – the extent to which the process becomes a part of the development of all individuals in proximity to the school – not merely the permitting of adult basketball games in the gym during the evening hours.

As well, it takes no crystal ball or a Wright Report to know that adult education will expand dramatically, replacing our present obsession with adolescent schooling.

By the end of the decade, it will be obvious that the time and energies of people can no longer be diverted to the economic growth syndrome – the production of goods, the necessary mining of the planet's limited resources and the resultant pollution of the earth's air and water Thus, the replacement of the value placed on material goods with a concern for human development appears to be the only rational alternative.

The end of the existing association of age and schooling will encourage many patterns of learning. Young people will leave school in their 'teens – to indulge in other educational activities which may look something like the Opportunities for Youth Program – and return to more formal learning arrangements later in life. And, one may hope, the end of continuous and isolated schooling will encourage a community commitment to learning which will be expressed through the use of television, and the educational programs provided as part of their role by private industry and the service sector of our society.

It is to these tasks that we should address ourselves particularly in the preparation of teachers who can cope with this expanded role, in the provision of buildings with a capacity for a variety of future educational uses, and in the developing of structures to co-ordinate the social, recreational as well as educational impulses of our society.

* * *

Ontario's Educative Society must be judged first as a unique collection of extremely valuable materials for any individual who's anxious to comprehend the Ontario educational establishment. Volume 1, the expansion of the educational system, examines some of the major challenges of the Sixties and Seventies, briefly expresses a balanced point of view and then proceeds to assault the reader with a barrage of factual and statistical information on the characteristics of the Ontario population, enrolment in schools, universities and colleges, the characteristics of teachers and the financial realities in this prosperous province. Statistical charts and maps abound and perhaps a more complete record of the essential data has not been gathered and presented more meaningfully and attractively.

The second volume, entitled "The administrative structure", examines the complicated development of the financing arrangements for elementary, secondary and post-secondary institutions which seem now to have risen to preeminence in the thinking of those involved with budget ceilings and monetary accountability. In this section, the story of the creation of the county boards is presented with precision, if not passion. As well, the never-ending activities within the various departments of both federal and provincial governments are presented in awesome detail.

The third volume in the series, entitled simply "Schools, Pupils and Teachers" will no doubt be the most popular volume. A most instructive historical analysis of the aims of education in Ontario forms the first chapter, followed by a detailed description of the organization and administration of schools and their programs. Perhaps the chapter on the role of measurement and evaluation merits special attention as it is an area in which the author feels so much at home. This volume contains some of Fleming's most pungent observations about the dangers of large schools, burgeoning administrations and the tragedy of poor teachers – suggesting that no school at all could probably be better than the imposition of an inept and uncommitted instructor. His statement that S.E.F. schools "showed how very substantial savings might result from mass purchase of components and supplies, without sacrificing individuality," has turned out to be a very poor prediction of the experiment.

Those who are exercised over the Wright Report will find comfort and solace in Volume IV, "Post-secondary and Adult Education". In the clear concise style which permeates every page of this monumental work, Fleming outlines the tortuous path which universities have trod in the past ten years towards greater cooperation among themselves and with the government and its agencies. It is perhaps the most outrageous aspect of the notorious Wright Report that it is totally unhistorical. There is an assumption that nothing much has been accomplished in this difficult process of achieving "collective autonomy" – and that the whole experiment should be swept aside to be replaced by a coordinating board (i.e. a provincial governing body). Fleming's book may provide the faint of memory with strength of heart in the days ahead.

The sixth and seventh volumes will concentrate on "Significant Developments in Local School Systems" and the "Educational Contribution of Associations".

Sometimes Fleming buries the reader in factual information and there are times when after foraging through another mountain of statistics one is led to ask: So what? As well, there are times when one suspects that reliance on statistics has led the author to assume that if there are no data there is no story. More teacher reminiscences, more student reactions could have broadened and humanized the account. But Fleming is master of the understatement and the tongue in cheek. Referring to the expansion of administration activities in the Sixties he observes that it "caused misgiving in some quarters" and in spite of rising female expectations, he remarks that the highest administrative positions in education "were, of course, largely restricted to men." And the framework of reality over idealism is established in the first volume with the statement that "the role of the schools and colleges as unemployment relief agencies should not be discounted."

*   *   *

After one has put down these volumes one is disposed to ask: Were there any alternatives? Will Bill Davis go down in history as a great Minister of Education because he was perceptive of the major directions, rode the mainstream, and convinced his Cabinet colleagues that educational expansion should be paramount? Certainly these were his achievements and deserve acclaim. However, during the years I watched his performance, I never failed to admire his *political* finesse – the very attributes which have been given full flight in his rôle as Premier. He gathered good people about him, took their advice, protected them from attacks, made their battles his own. In return, he received their warm loyalty, to such an extent that the arm's length relationship which should exist between civil servants and the elected government disappeared. To some extent, the priorities in spending seemed to ride not only with the particular enthusiasm of the Minister, but with the relationship between Davis and the particular individual who favoured, let us say, E.T.V. or educational research. The disadvantages in this state of affairs are obvious.

A similar closeness between the executives of teacher and trustee organizations dissipated any differences as easily as the smoke which floated across the Davis desk from the ministerial cigar. Education, in Ontario, became totally non-political. There will be those who would applaud the isolation of learning from rotten, dishonest politics and politicians, but it happens that schools are in the public sector and that policies affecting the direction of the educational system should be hammered out in meaningful debate. This simply never happened. With a smile of friendly goodwill, every criticism was treated by Bill Davis and his associates as a kind of playful exercise of the opposition role. Never was there a substantive reply in matters of educational philosophy – never a tough assessment about priorities and how important these priorities were to the nature of our society.

Again and again, with monotonous regularity Tim Reid, the Liberal education critic, appealed for a major thrust in compensatory education in the early years for those children who were economically disadvantaged. Each speech was greeted with platitudinous rejoinders of common agreement on the justice of the cause – but never was there a debate on the fact that without such a program the central slogan of the Davis years – equality of education – was a fraud.

Bill Davis never considered himself an educationist, but he knew that he was a master tactician. He disrupted his opposition by that disarming pose that he was a simple Brampton boy, who had struggled through high school, played football and, though not a scholar, was one of those solid, practical, second-class honour students who are the mainstay of our society. This is the image which led to his leadership victory and his election success – but he is far more. He can be perfectly clear on any issue he wishes, or he can circumvent clarity with prize-winning examples of political obtuseness. He knows exactly what he is doing and his sense of timing is superb. Intervention in the affairs of school boards or universities is always a potentially danger-ous move, but Davis would wait it out until his intervention was conceived to be the only solution to both sides, then, quietly, in a private conference, the issue was resolved. No triumphs. No humiliations. Faces saved all around.

His capacity for delay was monumental. For two years, the financing of secondary education for separate schools festered. Davis kept cool, never moving one way or the other. Then, just before an election, when any profound debate would be buried and, indeed, when any reply on the subjct would be considered "partisan", the decision was made. And in the process, the whole controversy over school costs, a controversy in which the new Premier was particularly vulnerable, was lost in the debate on separate schools.

Fleming views Davis as a remarkable technocrat-politician with his heart in the right place, and there is much truth in this view. But Canadians may come to see their future Prime Minister as an intelligent, calculating, careful individual who learned his lessons in the John A. Macdonald tradition – in the offices of the Ontario Department of Education.

No one will claim that Fleming's *Ontario's Educative Society* is the last word on the state of schooling and learning in the 1960's. Few will dispute that it is a valuable and helpful work on an important subject and a skilful politician. Both will be the source of continuing interest and debate in the 1970's.

Revolution and Education in Quebec

Norman Henchey

Although we should be cautious about using "revolutionary" to describe social change, the word does seem to apply naturally to the developments which have taken place in Quebec since 1960. The political, economic, and cultural events of the Quiet Revolution are well known but if we are to understand the meaning of Quebec in 1970 we must see these events as manifestations of a fundamental shift in the consciousness of a people – in the sense of identity and in the values and aspirations which arise from this consciousness. Where it was once customary to define the French-speaking Quebecer in terms of his attachment to tradition, his loyalty to the Church, his elitist view of society, his distrust of change, and his detachment from the economic concerns of the continent, the new definition is in terms of a concern for the present and future, adherence to a secular and political ethic, an egalitarian view of society, a commitment to change, and a search for economic control. If *la survivance* remains the prime goal of Quebec society, the search is now taking place in Hydro-Québec not Ste-Anne-de-Beaupré, and the leaders are technocrats and anii-mateurs not priests and notaries.

The revolution has touched every aspect of Quebec society but no institution has undergone a more penetrating and far-reaching transformation than education. This has been true for both theoretical and practical reasons. Quebec has always taken philosophy seriously and from the beginning of the 1960's it was recognized by those who led the reform that the new social, economic, and political courses which were being plotted had to be translated into new goals, structures, institutions, and processes for the educational system. Out of this philosophical necessity was created the Parent Commission with its open mandate to investigate education in the Province and to make recommendations for change. At a practical level, if the Quiet Revolution was to be realized, a more highly educated and trained population would be required and the responsibility for ensuring this had to be in the hands of those who were orchestrating the aspects of the reform. Out of this need came the Ministry of Education.

When the Liberals came to power in 1960 they inherited an educational system with unique characteristics. Public education was divided into two parallel and autonomous sectors, one Catholic and predominantly French, the other Protestant and predominantly English. At the provincial level power resided in a Catholic Committee and a Protestant Committee each responsible for the administration, curriculum, examinations, and certification of teachers within its domain. At the local level there were over 1,700 Catholic and Protestant school boards. Outside of this public system there was a large variety of private schools, mostly convents and collèges classiques, as well as government institutions (écoles normales, écoles de métiers, and so on) under the jurisdiction of over a dozen ministries. English-speaking students (in the Protestant sector and in English schools in the Catholic sector) could go directly from public secondary schools to university but, although there existed French secondary schools, the normal route to university for French-speaking students was through the private collèges classiques, a rigorous humanities-oriented program which took eight years of study beyond the elementary school level.

During the fifties there was certainly criticism of specific educational problems but the underlying assumptions appeared to be satisfactory – for the Church, for those concerned about the preservation of French language and culture, for the political and social elite, for taxpayers, for the English, for those who wished to keep politics and education separate. But if this education was in harmony with the style of the fifties it was discordant with the new goals of the sixties. The collèges classiques and the French-language universities were not producing adequate numbers of qualified personnel in the new areas of priority: management, science, engineering, and technology. Access to university was limited. The drop-out rate was the highest in Canada. Structures were complex and over-centralized. There was no coordination among various sectors: Catholic and Protestant, public and private.

* * *

When Paul Gérin-Lajoie became Minister of Youth in 1960, he took three steps to ensure that education would be caught up in the dynamics of the new era in Quebec. First, he assumed financial control of public education. Second, he engineered the creation of the Royal Commission of Inquiry on Education. Third, he focused his efforts on secondary education; in a flurry of legislation he extended the age of compulsory attendance to fifteen and established a framework within which school boards could cooperate with one another to make public secondary education more extensive and comprehensive. He followed this up by "Operation 55" which created 55 Catholic and 9 Protestant regional school boards to provide secondary education.

The second phase of the educational reform came in 1963 when the Parent Commission produced the first volume of its design for reform. Its central recommendation was the creation of the post of Minister of Education. This was a crucial point in the development of the reform; reformers saw it as essential for the integrated reorientation of the society and at the same time it was a direct and fundamental challenge to the existing structures and traditions. There was a great deal of philosophical and emotional discussion on the question and when Bill 60 was finally passed in 1964 it was after several compromises and a good deal of hard selling. In addition to the creation of the post of Minister of Education, the law provided for an advisory body called the Superior Council of Education to act as counterpoint to the Department of Education and two Committees, one Catholic and one Protestant, to make regulations in the specific areas of moral and religious education. The Government was now in effective control of education and the power of religious authorities was reduced to precise limits.

The third phase of the reform came in the fall of 1964 when the Parent Commission published Volumes II and III of its report. The Commission proposed a detailed plan for the reform of education from kindergarten through university. Its recommendations included an "activist" orientation for elementary schools, comprehensive secondary education with subject promotion, post-secondary "institutes" to complete general education and to prepare for university studies and technological occupations, and more specialized university programs. In general, the reaction to the vision of the Commission was one of awe and enthusiasm. Through 1965 and 1966 the mechanics of translating recommendations into realities were explored and the reorganization of elementary and secondary education got under way.

If there was a certain self-assurance, by the beginning of 1966, about the direction and rhythm of the reform, there were some indications, by the end of the same year, that this confidence might have been premature. In the elections of June 1966 the Liberals were defeated by the National Union party and many attributed this defeat to a feeling in the electorate that the "politique de grandeur" was going too far too fast. Almost at the same time, Volumes IV and V of the Parent Report were made public. The Commission recommended unified school boards responsible for all education – English and French, Catholic, Protestant, and nonconfessional – in a particular territory, with Committees in each school to determine its confessional nature and Councils of School Development to coordinate school boards in an economic region. If consensus formed around previous recommendations of the Commission, the public was badly divided on the question of unified school boards. This issue was to ferment and grow as questions of administration, politics, religion, and language became entangled and the splits in the society became visible.

As polarization began to develop over school boards, a new ingredient, confrontation, was introduced in a struggle between the government and the teaching profession. During the Sixties, the teaching force had been growing in size, competence, and confidence; at the same time the bills for the educational reform were starting to come in. To control costs, the government provided "guidelines" to school boards negotiating contracts with teachers. In late 1966 and early 1967 wave after wave of strikes brought the educational system virtually to a halt. The government passed legislation ordering the teachers back to work, imposing a single salary scale for most teachers in the Province, and establishing a framework for collective bargaining at the provincial rather than local level. The results of this struggle were that the government strengthened its control over expenditures. In future the arena for negotiating teachers' salaries and working conditions would be provincial rather than local, and teachers were now de facto civil servants.

Meanwhile, a new crisis was developing, this time in post-secondary education. The reforms of elementary and secondary education were beginning to pay off: there were more students in school and they were staying longer. Something had to be done to coordinate and expand post-secondary education. In June 1967, the National Assembly passed a law establishing Collèges d'Enseignement Général et Professionnel or CEGEP's as they came to be called. A network of these public, free, and comprehensive institutions was established, offspring of the marriage of écoles normales, instituts de technologie, and collèges classiques. A great deal was riding on the CEGEP experiment: the rationalization of post-secondary education, the provision of equal access to advanced studies, a balance between pre-university and technical programs. The promises and realities were hard to reconcile and in the fall of 1968 demonstrations, strikes, and occupations closed the CEGEP's. When the orgy of self-examination was spent, they reopened, their ideals and vitality largely intact but somewhat more mature. But the relentless pace of development soon posed a new question: What to do with the graduates of the CEGEP's? The answer was the Université du Québec, a public multi-campus university built on *modules* of professors and students. The momentum was picking up, the crises were being resolved, and the educational system seemed to be holding together – more or less.

* * *

By the end of 1968 the basic political and structural changes had been made in the educational system: the Ministry of Education had been established and was directing the reform with a good deal of power and success; large, comprehensive regional high schools were springing up throughout the Province; CEGEP's were established to receive the graduates of these secondary schools and the Université du Québec would soon be ready to complete the public system; the Government was beginning to control school board expenditures and the teaching profession had been reorganized by fiat. There remained the problem of school boards. There were over 1,000 boards in the Province, Catholic and Protestant. Planners were anxious to reduce the number and the religious division seemed no longer appropriate to many people, in view of the pluralism and secularism which had been growing through the Sixties. At first sight it looked like a relatively simple issue but it became exceedingly complicated as the implications began touching the root nerves of the society. First, the basic division in Quebec was no longer Catholic-Protestant but French-English, yet the constitutional protection of minority rights in education covered religion, not language. Second, the traditional relationship between the two groups had been cultivated by their isolation from each other; the Quiet Revolution broke down this isolation as the French developed an integrated concept of Quebec as a whole and as the English were increasingly reminded of their minority status by being "coordinated" into unified structures. What the English saw as "rights" the French saw as "privileges". Third, as the self-consciousness of the French shifted from historical to social-economic-political expression they began to see more clearly the magnitude of the threat to their survival as a people, even in Quebec. Nor was their anxiety eased by the knowledge that the birth rate in Quebec had dropped below the national average and that 90 per cent of immigrants to the province were opting for English education.

Within this context it was becoming increasingly clear that on the one hand, unified school boards were essential to the French if the integrity of the revolution was to be preserved and, on the other, an English-French division of school boards was essential to the English if their education was to preserve at least some measure of the power and identity it had formerly enjoyed. The drama of St. Léonard, acted out on national television and in the streets of Montreal and the massive McGill Français march, both in 1969, increased the polarization and raised the temperature of the language question.

The National Union government, badly divided on the issue, created a Royal Commission on Linguistic Rights but it was evident that events in the Province would not slow to the measured pace of a Commission and some immediate action would have to be taken. In the fall of 1969 the government attempted a balancing act. The first part was Bill 63 designed to promote French as the working language of the Province, to give parents the right to choose English- or French-language instruction for their children, and to strengthen the teaching of French in English schools. The debate was intense, the English went along with the idea, French groups took to the streets in protest, and the Bill was passed by the National Assembly. The second part of the package was Bill 62 which was intended to replace the forty-odd Catholic and Protestant school boards on the Island of Montreal by eleven unified boards with parents' committees for each school and a single appointed council for the whole Island to coordinate services and resources. This Bill provoked strong English opposition and died in committee as the Assembly was dissolved for elections. In April 1970, Bourassa and the Liberals came to power; with the trauma of the October crisis and the search for 100,000 jobs, it was the summer of 1971 before another attempt was made to do something about school boards. Two bills were introduced; the first reorganized school boards off the Island of Montreal, reducing the 800 boards to fewer than 200 and keeping the confessional division. It passed easily. The second bill provided for unified school boards in Montreal, following the general pattern of the previous attempt, but including safeguards for minority representation. English reaction was vocal and hostile; notice was served that the constitutionality of the bill would be challenged in the courts and the principle of unified school boards was assailed in public meetings and in print. On the other side, the Parti Québécois members of the National Assembly demanded revision of the language protections of Bill 63 and launched a filibuster. Unable to walk between the furies, the government backed off and the two solitudes continued to glare at each other in limbo.

*   *   *

Looking back over the last twelve years of Quebec education, it is easy to see the successes of the revolution in education: public responsibility for the development of education in the person of a Minister, the streamlining of structures, impressive buildings, massive investments, new vitality in old institutions and the creation of new institutions, more highly qualified teachers, freer access to schooling from kindergarten through university, less inequality from one region to another, improved programs with more choices, freer and more creative spirit in schools, closer relationship between school and society.

It is also possible to identify some broad trends, the implications of which may not always be too clear. The first of these trends has to do with the concentration and diffusion of power. In one sense the revolution marked a shift of power from some groups (mainly the Church) to the government and, at the early stages, the reform seemed to be looking for some balance in the distribution of educational power. Yet over the past twelve years financial and general policy-making power has continued to collect around the Department of Education as the Church withdrew, as the Superior Council was unable to establish its credibility as a balancing agency, as school boards increased their dependence on the government, and as the focus for planning and coordination and the arena for solving problems became the Province as a whole. The government has seemed determined to remain the custodian of the vision of reform and the director of its implementation, but increasingly there are signs that it may be losing control. The most obvious is the growing strength, syndicalism, and political radicalism of the teaching profession; it is difficult to predict the effects of diverging ideological and economic views between government and teachers but we cannot lightly dismiss the effects on the development of education of a sustained and fundamental conflict between the two. A second source of the erosion of government power is the spirit of freedom and participation which has spread through Quebec education. Initially, freedom and participation were imposed on the system by government regulation but now participation and initiative by local administrators, teachers, students, and (finally) parent and community groups are becoming widespread in matters related to curriculum, textbook selection, methods, and the organization of schools. Local initiative in specifics is coming into collision with government control of general policy and resources. A balance between centralization and decentralization has yet to be achieved.

A second general trend is that, while the influence of

Catholicism in Quebec society and education has drastically declined, philosophical and ethical concerns remain central. Marxist dialectic may be replacing scholastic syllogisms, the animateur may be replacing the priest, and social activism may be replacing missionary zeal, but a thread of the ideal runs from education in the age of Duplessis to education in the age of Bourassa.

A third trend is that the educational system in Quebec is beginning to experience the problems found in systems elsewhere. Quebec is spending about $1.5 billion a year on education and the money is beginning to get scarce as social welfare, health services, and the other demands of a complex society increase their claims on the public purse. Ever-increasing numbers of teachers are competing for a shrinking number of jobs. Large secondary schools, particularly in the urban areas, are beginning to experience the *angst* of alienation, indifference, bad trips, and violence once associated only with the schools of New York. The promise of Education Weeks, "Stay in School and Earn More Money!", is becoming harder to realize as high school dropouts, electro-technologists and political science majors stand together in unemployment lines.

Finally, the contradictions of the social and educational revolution are becoming sharply defined. The French are a majority in Quebec and a minority in North America; the English are a minority in Quebec but dominate elsewhere. Cultural ties with France notwithstanding, the educational reforms have Americanized the system: comprehensive high schools à la James B. Conant; CEGEP's like junior colleges; the Université du Québec, the University of California; la Corporation des Enseignants du Québec, the American Federation of Teachers; le *leadership*; programmed budgeting. Many of the leaders of the educational reform are graduates, not of the Sorbonne, but of Alberta, Columbia, Stanford, and Harvard. If the medium is the message (and the massage) can the message of Quebec survive the medium of the James Bay Power Project, translated technology manuals, behavioural objectives, Sesame Street, and accountability?

If the aspiration of Quebec education in 1960 was to get out from under the thumb of a rural curé, the irony of Quebec education in 1972 is to avoid becoming a well-oiled ball-bearing in the machine model of North American technology and empire. And it may just make it, for in many ways the culture of Quebec is in tune with the counter-culture elsewhere: reflective, organic, committed, and community-centred. Philosophy, science, art, and humanity continue to interact in Quebec as they do few places elsewhere. In 1971 the Minister of Education, Guy Saint-Pierre, an engineer, called for the de-schooling of schools. In 1972 the Minister of Education, François Cloutier, is a psychiatrist. The revolution in Quebec education is by no means finished.

Current Developments in Education in Atlantic Canada

Peter McCreath

If there are general trends in educational development in
Atlantic Canada, they do not seem remarkably different
from those in other parts of Canada, though there are some
noteworthy exceptions.

There is general concern about the rising cost of education,
and about the increasing percentage of the tax dollar con-
sumed by education. This has led recently to the complete
reorganization of the school systems in New Brunswick and
Prince Edward Island, and to the establishment of a major
Royal Commission in Nova Scotia. In both New Brunswick
and Prince Edward Island, the financing of elementary and
secondary education has been taken over directly by the
respective provincial governments, and the number of school
districts has been reduced drastically. Particularly in the
case of Prince Edward Island, this was a long overdue step.
Prior to reorganization, there were more school trustees
than teachers in Prince Edward Island. The number of school
districts there has been reduced from over 400 to 5.

In the short run, these reorganizations caused considerable
discontent, particularly among local politicians who subsequently found themselves returned to the humble status
of ordinary citizens. It is believed that reorganization had
a great deal to do with the defeat of the Robichaud government in New Brunswick. However, now that a couple of
years have passed, people generally seem reconciled to the
new and logically more efficient system, although it is as

yet too soon to estimate any long-term effect.

* * *

The appointment of a Royal Commission under Dr. John F. Graham of the Dalhousie Department of Economics was one of the first acts of the Regan government after taking office in Nova Scotia in October, 1970. The Commission report is expected some time in 1973. Both the appointment of the Royal Commission and the attitude and stance of the government of Nova Scotia during a protracted teachers' salary dispute earlier this year, seem to suggest that the Liberals feel that concern about the cost of education and, more particularly, opposition to the property school tax, were major factors in their stunning and totally unanticipated electoral victory of 1970. During the dispute, nothing could have been clearer than that the government believed that public sympathy was totally on their side.

In January 1972, after 4 months of negotiating, the government announced a 5 per cent guideline on salary increases for persons paid out of provincial coffers. Had this been followed across the board, the government might have been able to make it stick. But, despite many semantical explanations by the Minister of Finance (who by surprising coincidence happened also to be the Minister of Education), both teachers and civil servants refused to lie down and play dead when, for example, medical practitioners were permitted to raise their fees under medicare by 20 per cent. At about the same time the government also announced an increase in provincial income tax which would have the effect of immediately absorbing any 5 per cent raise. The average teacher would be left even further behind in relation to the ever-increasing cost of living. Moreover, the teachers insisted that they should get some compensation for the five days that the government arbitrarily added to the school year.

Towards the latter stages of the dispute, the teachers resorted to a variety of sanctions such as work-to-rule, walkouts, and, what ultimately proved to be most success-ful, discontinuance of all extra-curricular activities. The latter seemed to be the straw that broke the camel's back; it was the issue that aroused the students and led to student protests of various sorts both for and against the teachers, but generally against the government. This in turn seemed to arouse the parents, and it soon became clear that public opinion had shifted from support of the government to recog-nition that the teachers would not back down and to a general desire for compromise and settlement.. (In the end a settlement was reached whereby the teachers got a 7.6 per cent raise (5% plus 2.6% for the extra five days, but the government was able to save face by saying it was only a 5 per cent raise.)

While the dispute meant an unsettled and at times trau-matic year in most Nova Scotia schools and demonstrated the cynicism of the provincial government, the whole incident had a significant impact on the teachers of the province, both collectively and individually. The dispute fostered unity amongst teachers. There was a substantial increase in direct teacher participation in the activities of the Nova Scotia Teachers' Union. It had been over a decade since Nova Scotia teachers had been involved in a major dispute, and there is nothing like a salary fight to get people involved. The conflict had the effect of causing many people in the province to re-assess the role of the teacher in society, to recognize that the old stereotype of the teacher had changed. It was a year during which more teachers asked more questions about their job, their future and their role in society than ever before.

*   *   *

Newfoundland is the Atlantic Province perhaps most in need of major change in the organization of the school system. With the exception of the Faculty of Education at Memorial University, educational change and innovation, seems to be somewhere between non-existent and barely noticeable in Newfoundland. The explanation for this state of affairs, as with most things in Newfoundland, seems to lie with religion and politics. In Newfoundland one can still be denied a teaching position in a publicly supported school owing to one's religion. In fact, this past spring the House of Assembly considered the case of an otherwise qualified teacher-applicant who was denied a position because she refused to state her religious affiliation. It was decided that the House was powerless to do anything about it.

Religion is endemic to the Newfoundland school system. Within every school district, there are five school boards and five school systems for each of the major religious denominational groups: Roman Catholic, Pentecostal, Salvation Army, Anglican and United. Combined with this is probably the most elaborate and hierachial system of patronage and government appointment of office holders in the country.

Possibly much of this will change under the new régime of Premier Frank Moores, a man whose greatest political asset has been his extraordinary organizational ability. Since entering politics in 1968, Moores has repeatedly expressed the view that many of Newfoundland's problems could be overcome, if her citizens were given the opportunity of a good education. Whether or not this is true, under Moores one would expect to see a complete reorganization of the school system, the establishment of many more vocational schools, institutes of technology and possibly a number of community schools.

*   *   *

One important trend in education in the Atlantic area is the increasing attention being paid to the provision of special education programs and facilities for particular groups and types of children. More variety and flexibility is available for all students and those with learning problems are getting much more support. The Atlantic Institute of Education (about which more below) is taking a lead in providing programs for special education teachers, but the demand far exceeds what it can supply.

A particularly interesting experiment in this general area, though at the post-secondary level, is the Transition Year Program (TYP) of Dalhousie University. Unique in Atlantic Canada, the program began as an attempt to increase the opportunities for native Blacks and Indians to attend university. Initially, the programs sought students between the ages of 17 and 24 who had dropped out of high school somewhere between grades IX and XII, and gave them some intensive training in language, math, history and science, and in the skills essential to success at university, such as reading and note-taking. Students accepted for the program, which has now been in operation two years, are fully supported financially and receive special tutoring for one year. The immediate objective is to prepare students, in one year, for regular attendance in one of the Dalhousie programs.

More recently, however, standards of admission have been upgraded. Applicants are expected now to have completed some grade XII subjects. "We have found," said Dr. P. A. Pillay, Director of the Program and Associate Professor of History at Dalhousie, "that not all drop-outs want to go to university." Students who drop out of high school do so for many reasons. Therefore, because of the limited space, funds and facilities, and the abundance of applicants, the TYP now accepts only those who have demonstrated the desire and ability to achieve in a formal learning situation.

As yet, it is too soon to assess the achievements of Dalhousie's TYP. As Dr. Pillay has pointed out, many problems and tensions develop when you integrate Whites, Blacks and Indians into the same classrooms. Having been exiled from his native South Africa for his opposition to racial discrimination, and being of East Indian origin, Dr. Pillay has been in an excellent position from which to get the TYP off the ground.

Involvement of representatives of the Black and Indian communities has not been as active as initially intended owing to the conflicts between the various sections and associations within the Black and Indian communities. However, recently the Black Education Committee, organized by the Blacks themselves, and consisting of representatives of the various Black organizations, has agreed to monitor the programs and advise on its content and aims.

Along with this increased concern for providing for the needs of individual or exceptional children and young adults, there is a general tendency toward the decentralization of curriculum planning. Gone is the day when the provincial department of education defined the curriculum, sent out a textbook in September ,and administered a central departmental examination in June. In all parts of the Maritimes, greater liberty in course planning and development is being gvien to school boards, and more particularly to individual schools and teachers.

There are several visible manifestations of this trend: consolidation of schools and school districts, the abolition of provincial examinations, the availability of more funds for pilot projects and curriculum development within the schools, the movement toward the adoption of credit systems. Although many such manifestations are new to the Maritimes, they are not new to curriculum development and educational planning and programming in Canada. Thus the problems encountered there are not unique to this area, though finding enough money is always a greater problem in the Maritimes

While the departments have been willing to permit teachers and schools an increasing degree of latitude in planning, they have not, with but one exception, been prepared to recognize that more teacher planning necessarily requires that time be allocated or scheduled out of the classroom for such work. The ice has been broken in this regard in New Brunswick where in their most recent contract the government has granted teachers a certain allocation of days which can be used for individual in-service. Also, the New Brunswick government has established a Committee on Grants for Innovation, and funded it on the basis of $9.00 per teacher per year, which amounts to approximately $75,000 a year. In effect, funds are available to teachers who wish to experiment with their own ideas, in the same way that funds are available for government sponsored pilot projects. Still, innovation costs money, and the basic problem in bringing about change is finding the money to pay for it.

Owing to the size and proximity of the Atlantic provinces, and to the recent establishment of the Maritime Council of Premiers, one might expect to find considerable cooperation in education. Hitherto, this has not been the case. Maritime Union is just as far away with respect to schools, universities, departments and teachers' unions as in anything else. There is a council of teachers federations of the four Atlantic provinces, but this year it did not even meet. Some glimmer of hope for cooperation might be seen in the social studies council on curriculum, which met this past June in Charlottetown. It is as yet too soon to tell what might result from this.

The one really successful example of Atlantic cooperation in education has been Project Atlantic Canada, set up by the Canada Studies Foundation. The purpose of the project is both the production of materials and the understanding of the processes of teaching within the broad theme of cultural diversity and regionalism. It is concerned with curriculum and methodology. It seeks better ways of learning and teaching Canadian concepts and concerns, how and at what levels these concerns can be studied, and what materials and methods must be used.

There are, in fact, four projects within Project Atlantic Canada (one bringing together teachers in Newfoundland/Labrador, a second based in New Brunswick, a third joint P.E.I./Nova Scotia project, and a fourth involving Francophone teachers in the Maritimes), each of the four being autonomous in defining its themes and projects within the main theme, under a coordinating committee representing all four groups. Never before has such a large scale curriculum project involving teachers and students been attempted in Atlantic Canada. Although a teachers' project, it has had the effect of bringing the four departments and the four teachers' federations into close cooperation as never before. In fact, Project Atlantic Canada cannot work without their close cooperation.

Aside from inducing cooperation within the four provinces, it can be expected to have several positive benefits for Atlantic Canada. Above all, it will mean teacher and student involvement in the process of curriculum development and building. At the present time, there are in excess of 200 teachers in Atlantic Canada involved as key team members. With the spillover effect, literally thousands of teachers and students will be directly or indirectly involved within a year.

In addition, there will be other benefits. Materials and methods developed in Atlantic Canada will be used to educate students in other parts of the country about Atlantic Canada. Not unimportant either is the fact that the seed and support funds supplied by the Canada Studies Foundation will stimulate increased and cooperative financial contributions from Atlantic Region sources. We are willing to spend our own money, but it is satisfying to have a few Ontario dollars in the pot as well.

Perhaps the most promising development in education in Atlantic Canada of late has been the establishment of the Atlantic Institute of Education. Initially intended to coordinate and develop the resources of all the universities in Atlantic Canada in the general area of teacher education and educational research, the Atlantic Institute of Education was established by the government of Nova Scotia in 1969 but, as yet, none of the other three provinces have formally joined in its financial support and accepted a voice in its direction. Nevertheless, during its two years of operation under the direction of Dr. Joseph A. Lauwerys, the Atlantic Institute of Education already has a remarkable list of projects and achievements to its credit, and has attracted considerable research capital from other parts of Canada and the world.

Any examination of issues or developments in this region must always take into consideration two factors: first, that it is essentially a conservative and an economically disadvantaged region of the country, and therefore developments will usually tend to lag behind other richer and more prosperous areas. And second, that although small, close together, and similar, the Atlantic provinces cling to their individuality and separate existence; thus it is always dangerous to lump them together and look for common trends and developments. Although such things as Project Atlantic Canada and the Atlantic Institute of Education are both unique and exciting, the tendency in Atlantic Canada is to let the bulk of the experimenting and costly research be conducted by such wealthy provinces as Ontario and Alberta. Consequently, although progress is steady and continuous, Atlantic Canadians seem satisfied (if only because of financial necessity) to follow rather than to lead the way in educational development and innovation.

A Review of Some Recent Developments in Education on the Prairies

Jim Small, Robert Bryce, Gordon McIntosh

Saskatchewan: A Time For Testing

To understand the development of education in Saskatchewan it helps to view the province as an economic and political system shaped by similar forces as the other western provinces, yet unique in some respects. While there is no declared policy of emulation or conformity between Saskatchewan and Alberta there are obvious points of similarity in past and present developments which indicate a readiness to look beyond the border.

Parallels can be seen with respect to structural forms such as school divisions (Alberta) and larger school units (Saskatchewan); locally appointed Superintendents (optional in Saskatchewan); and regional decentralization of Supervisory Services (six regions each with a provincial Superintendent).

Similar trends exist in the selective decentralization of such interna as curriculum building, text book authorization and final examinations. The means of implementation differ however. In Saskatchewan decentralization is attempted at the high school level through a system of individual teacher accreditation. To apply for accreditation in a particular subject a teacher must meet certain formal course requirements in his basic qualifications, have a minimum of two year's teaching experience, and have completed an in-service program offered by the Saskatchewan Teachers' Federation. Accredited status empowers a teacher to set and mark his own matriculation examinations and grade his pupils.

Also at the high school level the new division IV program permits more flexibility in course offerings and choices by pupils. The requisite for high school graduation is five courses at each of the 10, 20 and 30 levels leaving six to be chosen freely from the school's program of courses. This innovation has been more favourably received in urban than in rural areas where the small high schools can offer fewer options.

A final illustration of the decentralization process involves both parents and pupils in the open attendance areas of Regina and Saskatoon in which a pupil may attend the high school of his choice, subject to sufficient accommodation being available. Combined with the accreditation of certain high school teachers and declining enrolments, this has produced a novel source of consumer power. High school pupils naturally may be expected to be drawn to particular schools where they are hopeful of maximum success. For many this means the kind of marks which enhance their prospects of university admission and scholarships. Both teachers and administrators are sensitive to this potent force and conscious of the need for improved coördination between schools and institutions of higher education. One proposed solution would be the adoption of national college entrance examinations.

At the 1972 Legislative Assembly an act was passed which established a new Department of Continuing Education headed by a Deputy-Minister to be responsible, under the authority of the Minister of Education, for all post-secondary, higher and adult education. While this design for unitary control is in accord with the theme of continuous or recurrent education and facilities coördination, the initial plan of the new department is to evolve its own support services and traditions which may have the effect of demarcating the major phases of recurrent education, but may also initiate a new wave of professionalism within the educational hierarchy of the province.

A priority concern of the deputy minister is the disposition of the report of the Minister's Advisory Committee on Community Colleges which is due by September. The committee has conducted extended hearings and briefings across the province, and has nurtured the government's theme of rural revitalization by means of community - based continuing education.

At the other end of the scale is the question of publicly supported kindergartens which has received extensive study during the past year. The report recommends that school boards be encouraged to establish publicly supported kindergarten programs, with provision of grant support to reflect the degree and type of implementation.

It might be anticipated therefore that these major thrusts in educational development will widen the scope of public involvement and add considerably to the education budget which already accounts for one third of the total public expenditure of the province. The dilemma facing the new government is how to find the means of satisfying an expectant public without overextending itself financially.

The root cause of the problem is Saskatchewan's depressed economy which appears to have evolved from too great reliance on primary commodities, especially wheat and potash, for which supply exceeds demand. A related cause is the population decline which is peculiar to Saskatchewan. These problems may be taken care of in the future by the process of natural growth, but in the meantime economies will be insisted upon at the public school level.

School finance programs have been changed to emphasize the pupil as the basic cost unit rather than the teacher. This measure may bring economic strictures and slow down the process of professionalization of the teaching force. At the same time the continuation of budget review procedures will act to impose ceilings and ensure a sharing of costs at a level satisfactory to the government.

The inevitable outcome of budget reduction plans are hostilities between teachers, trustees, and Departmental officers in their corporate forms. This is manifest in Saskatchewan in the area bargaining issue, an arrangement which was imposed by the government over the opposition of the Teachers' Federation. Meanwhile the proposal to institute a provincial salary system has been given the tacit support of the teachers but not the trustees. Tensions are evident while an undefended report is being prepared.

Another issue which may be cited as symptomatic of a general malaise is the Margaret Gordon vs. Moosomin School Unit Case in which the very structures and processes for decision making within the system have been questioned, including the authority of the Minister, the powers of the Board of Deference, and the rights of the school board and teacher.

In fairness to Saskatchewan it should be pointed out that conflict in education is a condition found across the nation – only the symptoms vary. The process of coming to terms will, however, be expedited by the development of informed leadership within the ranks of teachers, trustees and administrators.

This function is rightly that of the University of Saskatchewan through its faculties of education. Unfortunately the expansion of service to the profession is likely to be hindered by the threat to the existence of two independent faculties at Regina and Saskatoon occasioned by decreases in enrolment and reduced appropriations – up to 25 per cent in the case of the Regina faculty. Thus the present trends are likely to continue in Saskatchewan until the economy brightens or priorities are reässessed.

Manitoba And Separate Schools

"Once more unto the breech . . ."

At 5.18 a.m. on Thursday morning, July 20th, 1972, Manitoba's legislature completed its last item of business for the session by defeating a private member's resolution. The vote (30-22 with members from both sides breaking party ranks in the balloting) followed some five hours of heated debate.

Obviously this was no routine killing of non-government legislation for the private member who had advanced the resolution was none other than Premier Ed Schreyer (NDP). And the resolution? In essence it called for the legislature to establish a committee to study ways of increasing aid to Manitoba's 48 private and parochial schools. Denial of support for the resolution, a personal blow to Schreyer, was the latest event in Manitoba's continuing struggle with the question of public support for sectarian and private education.

Among the provinces only Manitoba, and to a much lesser degree, British Columbia, have failed to establish some sort of modus vivendi with regard to public assistance to "separate" schools.1 These arrangements vary from a "gentlemen's agreement" in Nova Scotia (especially Halifax and Sydney) where "Catholic schools" exist in practice but not in legislation, to legal provision for province-wide elementary and secondary separate schools as in Saskatchewan and Alberta. Throughout Manitoba's 102 years as a province the issue has flared and subsided and then flared again without resolution.

As was the case for its sister prairie provinces, Manitoba entered union under legislation which, while granting provincial jurisdiction over education guaranteed federal intervention in those instances where denominational schools which existed "by Law or practice at the Union" might be prejudicially affected by provincial regulations. Yet in 1890, in open contradiction of union legislation, the Manitoba Government assed the Public Schools Act which instituted a single, non-sectarian system to replace its then dual, Catholic-Protestant model.

The resulting furor inflamed secretarian and secular sensitivities througout Canada. The Conservative federal government of the day did attempt to redress Roman Catholic grievance only to fall victim to a "provincial rights" platform championed by Sir Wilfred Laurier's Liberals. The upshot was a clear victory for the Manitoba legislature but was called a "compromise" as a face-saving gesture. The single, non-secretarian system remained intact but a few wrinkles were added as a sop to the compromise. (One of these "wrinkles" was a clause which permitted ten or more French-speaking, or any non-English-speaking pupils in a given school to receive instruction in their mother language as well as exposure to English. By 1916 Manitobans had enough of what had become a near riot of non-English education[2] and the clause was repealed.)

But the question of support for private, and especially parochial, schools was far from settled. An entrenched Roman Catholic minority continued to press for rights similar to those enjoyed by their fellow adherents in Alberta and Saskatchewan. In 1965, Duff Roblin's Conservative government had eased some of this pressure – and generated some controversy[3] – through the introduction of a "shared services scheme" which gave non-public schools some access to public facilities.

In the early spring of 1972, Schreyer's declared intention to bring support to private and parochial schools set the debate boiling again throughout the province. Neither party loyalty nor conviction was sufficiently strong for a party policy to emerge. Lack of support within his own NDP ranks led Schreyer to threaten at one time in June to resign unless he received backing. Later he settled for sponsorship of a private member's resolution.

Opposite views in the debate were crystallized by two principals; Premier Schreyer, and Mines and Natural Resources Minister Sydney Green of the premier's own cabinet. In the finest tradition of parliamentary government, Green resigned from the Cabinet to fight the Premier's resolution, then returned to the cabinet after the debate.

Green argued that education must remain secular lest the public be forced to choose between which beliefs it would finance and which beliefs it would not. Separate schools, claimed Green, would sap the multicultural basis of public education. Further, schools should be concerned with teaching their charges how to think. What to think was more properly the concern of other institutions.4

Schreyer asked the legislature for a dispassionate, nonpartisan policy which would recognize the educational inequities which obtained in the absence of public support to parochial schools.5

Earlier in the year, advocates of Metro Winnipeg School reorganization had proposed the creation of parental committees which would be deeply and significantly involved in education at the institute level. It was clear that Schreyer favoured a close look at such expanded local control as a means of bringing separate and private schools under the larger public umbrella. Conceivably the special curriculum climate, and administration deemed desirable in separate schools might be obtained under the suzerainity of a parental committee imbued with the requisite philosophy. Of course it would be expected that the interests of other parental committees would ensure the appearance of an extremely diversified school system.

It remains now to be seen whether the defeat of Schreyer's resolution is also the kiss of death for the rather exciting prospect of parental committees. However, it would be wishful thinking at best to believe that the final word has been said on the separate school issue for Manitoba.

1. In the Manitoba situation "separate" is synonomous with Roman Catholic schools. While Schreyer's resolution included private schools, it was clear from the debate that the quintessential issue was over public support for denominational schools.
2. Mennonites, Ukranians, Poles, as well as French Manitobans demanded and received bilingual normal schools — financed from the public treasury.
3. Mines and Natural Resources Minister Syd Green of Manitoba's present NDP government called the conservative legislation a subterfuge for providing assistance to separate schools. (*Winnipeg Free Press*, July 7, 1972, p. 6)
4. *Loc.cit.*, p. 4
5. *Ibid.*

Alberta: The Reports Are In

The Time: *Friday, June 16, 1972*

The Place: *Auditorium of the Northern Alberta Institute of Technology in Edmonton*

The Event: *A closed-circuit, televised press conference to consider the just - released, much - heralded report of the Alberta Commission on Educational Planning which had been created three years earlier by Robert Clark, the aggressive, young Minister of Education in Premier Harry Strom's Social Credit administration, for purposes of developing a blueprint for education in Alberta to the year 2000.*

The Star Performers: *Dr. Walter Worth, Commissioner on Educational Planning; Lou Hyndman, Minister of Education; Jim Foster, Minister of Advanced Education; and Dr. Bert Hohol, Minister of Labour.*

So it was that a new era in Alberta education had its beginning, with Walter Worth (who two years before had been a vice-president at the University of Alberta and, prior to that, a professor and chairman of elementary education at the same institution) as the most influential figure in the emerging educational establishment, and the only holdover from the group of influentials who for the past ten years or more have largely determined the agenda for educational debate in Alberta.

Education in Alberta has undergone an astonishing change in the past year, not in current classroom practice but rather in the forward thrusts which gave promise of markedly affecting educational practices in the years ahead. It has been a year of dashed personal dreams for several persons who have given much to Alberta education as several key programs were eliminated by the new Conservative administration. It was a year of reports on education (three reports were released in late spring and early summer), and a year of as-yet-uncertain beginnings as charted by the Worth Commission.

Three major educational programs initiated by reform-minded leadership in the Social Credit government, beginning in 1967 with the "human resources" legislation of the Manning administration, were terminated or reshaped beyond recognition by Peter Lougheed's Conservatives.

First to go was the Alberta Human Resources Research Council. Created in 1967 by an Act of the Alberta legislature as a semi-independent crown agency, the Council had been given a very broad research mandate – "social, economic, educational and other research" related to the development of the human resources of Alberta. The Council from its inception was an awkward child (not really loved by any of its parents or prospective guardians).

First of all, it was a hybrid conceived by parents with very different sets of aspirations. The young idea men around Premier Manning had conceived the human resources program (and the resulting White Paper which figured prominently in the successful campaign for reëlection in 1967) as a means for putting a human face on a business-oriented, conservative provincial administration. At the same time the Alberta education establishment, spurred on by the creation of the Ontario Institute for Studies in Education and a desire to maintain a position of leadership in Canadian public education, was lobbying actively for the creation of an educational research agency supported generously by public funds.

The legislative result was HRRC which was to be an organization charged with responsibility for the full range of social research. From the outset the Council sailed stormy seas. The conservative factions in the Social Credit cabinet were never reconciled to the human resources ideology, nor could they see any useful purpose in a Council which at best was an expensive frill, at worst a dangerous agency which because of its semi-autonomy could embarrass the government. (This fear was amply confirmed in late 1970 when a Council report, *Social Futures* 1970-2005, prepared by Dr. Harold Dyck predicted diminished support for the Social Credit party in Alberta.)

By early 1972, some three years after Director Lorne Downey first assembled his staff, the Council seemed to have overcome its initial organizational problems and a steady stream of reports on various aspects of Alberta life was being released. Then the blow fell with Premier Lougheed's announcement that support for the Council would be discontinued. The funds released would be diverted to support for programs directly serving disadvantaged groups.

Why? Public statements by the Lougheed government gave no specific reasons for the decision. Perhaps the root cause was disillusionment with research and development as a means to social amelioration. The Conservatives have yet to come up with an alternative, although they have promised they will support educational improvement by better means of their own devising.

❂   ❂   ❂

Next on the chopping block were two more jewels in the Social Credit government's educational crown – the Innovative Projects Fund and Athabasca University. The Fund was a relatively minor, yet potentially very exciting, program created by Robert Clark early in his brief tenure as Minister of Education. Its purpose was to stimulate the trial and assessment of educational alternatives in local school systems throughout Alberta. Grants were to be made on the basis of educational rather than political criteria. Good proposals would be funded; poor ones, rejected.

Although there may have been some slippage in the basis for funding, the Fund unquestionably stimulated the search for improved educational practices at the grass-roots level (which, incidentally, HRRC did not). An outstanding example would be the support offered Calgary Separate's Bishop Carroll High School by the Fund in support of work in the areas of individualized learning and differentiated staffing. Without doubt Bishop Carroll represents a more human approach to secondary education. The Fund helped to make it happen.

Again the question: why was the Fund discontinued? The reasons are even more obscure and elusive than was the case for the Council. It was not a major drain on public funds. (The Council's yearly budget at no time exceeded eight hundred thousand dollars; the Fund was but a fraction of this.) One is driven to the somewhat cynical conclusion that, merits of programs aside, there are just very few votes to be gained by supporting programs of educational improvement. Lou Hyndman, Minister of Education in the Conservative cabinet, has promised an alternative to the Fund but this also has yet to be unveiled.

❋   ❋   ❋

Whereas HRRC and the Fund were terminated summarily, the Conservatives seem bent on making Athabasca University a particularly creative case study in institutional demise. Athabasca was brought into legal existence in early 1970, again under the leadership of Robert Clark as Minister of Education. The provincial government, in a White Paper on post-secondary education released at that time, stipulated a site for the university in the northwest suburbs of Edmonton near St. Albert and a program that would be limited to undergraduate studies in the arts and sciences, together with social science-related, undergraduate professional studies.

A Governing Authority was quickly appointed by the Cabinet. The Authority in turn invited Dr. Tim Byrne, then Alberta's deputy minister of education and a key figure in the creation of HRRC, to assume the Athabasca presidency. Within a year Byrne, working with a small staff, had developed the Athabasca concept.

Athabasca University was to be organized on the basis of "modules", in which teachers and students could come to know each other well and develop collegial working relationships. Instruction would be interdisciplinary, problem-centred, and related to the problems of the real world – pollution and urban concerns received special mention. (In passing one might note that Athabasca was to be sited in an idyllic, pastoral setting above the sleepy Sturgeon River some ten miles from the heart of the city.) Considerable emphasis was to be placed on modern, audiovisual learning technology and "systems" approaches to individualizing instruction.

Athabasca University, despite some sniping from its sister institution across the river, was recognized as a real step forward for Alberta post-secondary education. Nevertheless, in late spring, following a spate of rumours and denials, all of which seemed to originate from the office of Jim Foster, Minister of Advanced Education, the word came down: Athabasca University was dead. Or was it dead? Yes, Athabasca was "released" from its St. Albert site. Not in the forseeable future would a fourth university be built at this or any other site. No, the Governing Authority would not be dismissed nor would the staff be released.

Indeed, Athabasca University would go ahead as a "pilot project". Some two hundred students would be enrolled in the fall of 1973 for an experimental program modelled on the original Athabasca concept. The findings would be useful, Minister of Advanced Education Foster pointed out, whatever the fate of Athabasca as an institution.

Some of the reasons for the Athabasca decision are clear – declining enrolments and shortfalls in provincial revenues being the two most apparent. The reasons for the "pilot project" are more confusing. One surely does not have to keep an unneeded university on the books in order to encourage experimentation with alternatives in post - secondary education.

Some have speculated that the embryo Athabasca University will serve as the nucleus of an Open University for Alberta, using the full range of audiovisual communications media to bring education to the people of Alberta on a lifelong basis where they are with no institutional barriers.

❋   ❋   ❋

Just as this was the year of demise and slow strangulation of promising new programs in education begun under the Social Credit administration, so also was this the year of reports.

The first of these, the report of the Byrne Commission (yes, the same Byrne) struck to inquire into the administration and governance of Red Deer College may appear to be a parochial interest only. This is not the case – unless, of course, problems relating to the function and purpose of the community college as an institution are thought to be parochial concerns.

The basic facts of the situation can be sketched in quickly. Red Deer College is a publicly supported community college offering a range of programs at the post-secondary level with emphasis on academic transfer courses, to students in the central Alberta region. During the 1971-72 academic year, relationships between the senior administration and the college board on the one hand, and staff and students on the other, so deteriorated that the college was brought to a state of near collapse.

Urged on by the gravity of the situation and the embarrassment of a near disaster in an institution under his administrative jurisdiction located in his own constituency, Minister of Advanced Education Foster commissioned a public inquiry to be headed up by T. C. Byrne. The specific findings and recommendations brought forward by Byrne need not detain us. In brief the Colleges Act was suspended in its application to Red Deer College, the resignations of Board members and senior administration were accepted, an administrator was appointed to set matters straight, and the situation at the College is approaching normalcy.

The important aspects of the Red Deer case, however, are to be found in the root causes of the incident – namely, the absence of a suitable consensus among important College constituencies (the community at large, board members, students, instructional staff, and administrators) as to what the College is all about. Many see the College as a foot in the door to university status, and resist all efforts to make the institution as comprehensive in fact as it is in concept. Thus, in a real sense the College is more a junior university than a community-oriented institution devoted to a wide and balanced range of educational opportunities beyond the high school level.

In some degree, this state of uncertainty regarding goals prevails in each of Alberta's six public community colleges. These institutions, once uncritically heralded as the ready answer to a real need for expanded, comprehensive post-secondary educational services, seem to be beset by the same uncertainties, limited successes, and failures as affect the other bold educational thrusts of the seventies.

❋   ❋   ❋

No other province in Canada is under greater American influence than Alberta. Yet Alberta has a strong nationalist movement, strong enough to prompt Bob Clark in 1970 to appoint a "Committee of Inquiry into Non-Canadian Influence in Alberta Post-Secondary Education." Somewhat overdue (by perhaps a year) the report of the Committee was released this July. Chaired by Edmonton lawyer Arnold Moir and University of Alberta political scientist Richard Baird, the

Committee was charged with such tasks as discovering "the reason for the present distribution of non-Canadian personnel in the different sectors of Alberta post-secondary institutions," determining the "influence on Canadian content in programmes of study in Alberta post-secondary institutions," and suggesting "ways and means by which Alberta post-secondary institutions could develop a greater number of programmes of study having concern with, and application to, Canadian problems."

Beyond a diligent commitment to British spellings, the Moir-Baird report will of itself make little difference to post-secondary education in Alberta. Nor did it have to. The Committee in its concluding paragraph makes the wisest statement of its unjustifiably bulky presentation: "The Committee has been led to believe that the mere occurence (*sic*) of its hearings and deliberations has helped the search for satisfactory remedies of existing problems."

What does the report tell us about the current state of Canadianism in Alberta universities? We learn that 40 per cent of the academic staff of the University of Alberta do not hold Canadian citizenship, as compared with 43 per cent at the University of Lethbridge and 55 per cent at the University of Calgary. We learn also that there is considerable variation according to subject area. For example, some 61 per cent of arts faculty members hold citizenship other than Canadian as compared with 20 per cent of their physical education colleagues, the "worst" and "best" ratings respectively. Within arts faculties the anthropology/sociology, philosophy and political science faculties seem to be the worst offenders with 73, 70, and 67 per cents respectively of these faculty members holding citizenship other than Canadian.

What are we to do about this sorry state of affairs? Well, we can be very careful in the way we compose selection committees in order to discourage hiring through informal contacts with friends in graduate schools outside the country – the so-called "old boy network" (which in the Committee's view doesn't exist anyway). The Committee rejects quotas, favours advertising of positions, supports competence as the principal criterion in hiring, urges administrators not to ignore Canadian content in courses, shoots down the two-year tax concession for "visiting" professors, believes in motherhood, and generally speaking stands up for creative, courageous thinking in public inquiries.

Enough said.

*　　*　　*

On the basis of the indicators discussed above, one would be led to no other conclusion than that education in Alberta is a tired out, anaemic, stagnating enterprise. We have but one indicator to the contrary -- the report of the Committee on Educational Planning prepared by Dr. W. H. (Wally) Worth. With most other strong forces for development in Alberta education either snuffed out or preoccupied with internal organizational maintenance and survival, Worth's CEP report, *A Choice of Futures*, stands out in strong relief as the one positive thrust into the future currently influencing educational thought and action in Alberta.

The Commission on Educational Planning was initiated by Robert Clark as Minister of Education in 1969, as part of the progressive program promised by the supporters of Harry Strom in his campaign for the leadership of the Social Credit party in the fall of 1938. From the beginning it was seen as far more than a report on education. Influenced by the initial planning and conceptual work of Lorne Downey, who was later to become the coördinator of research for the Commission, CEP was strongly committed both to careful examination of the social/cultural context of the educational enterprise and to a future research perspective.

Worth's starting point in the CEP report is to develop the outline of two alternative social futures for Albertans, each of which is consistent with data derived from future forecasts. Worth then poses the question: what kind of future do Albertans want?

One of these futures, "second-phase industrial society," bears many similarities to Charles Reich's Consciousness II. It is the present extended into the future: economic values would continue to dominate, values "which lead to goals such as continuing expansion of goods, increased consumption which subordinates individual needs to the requirements of industry and technology."

By contrast Albertans have an opportunity to choose a future which in fundamental respects is discontinuous with the past. We can opt for what Worth calls a "person-centred" society, which is strongly reminiscent of Reich's Consciousness III. The characteristics, orientations, and values of a person-centred society would include "sensualism", "capacity for joy", "flexible structures that promote equal relationships", "interdependence", "coöperation", "humanism". Worth's own preference clearly is with his person-centred society.

This is pretty strong stuff in Alberta where rugged individualism is still regarded seriously as a virtue and Consciousness I personalities abound. The question then is: how does Worth hope to get away with it? Does he seriously believe that an educator and a report on education can be a means for the achievement of fundamental social reform?

Worth has spoken as follows of the dilemma he faces as a freely confessed reformer:

What this leads you back to is, first, to establish goals and ideals, which in themselves might be thought by some people to be revolutionary; then, to propose means of achieving those which are evolutionary, based on some perception of tolerable levels of change at a particular point in time; and then to build in the idea that you need to have some mechanism for self-renewal and continuing assessment.

His strategy is clear. Stimulate public debate on the fundamental shape of social life desired by Albertans. Recommend some specific changes which get the reform rolling. And make sure that mechanisms get built into the system so that reform is continuous.

Worth finds the means to these ends largely in two bodies of technique: educational planning and modern audio-visual communications media. The creation of a planning unit with real teeth within reorganized Departments of Education and Advanced Education, the establishment of an Alberta Academy akin in many respects to Britain's Open University, and the inauguration of an Alberta Communications Centre for Educational Systems and Services are illustrative of the approach that Worth would use.

It is far too early to gauge the likely effects of the Worth Report on Alberta education. Because it was released just prior to the summer doldrums, intensive public debate is not likely to begin until the autumn. Major legislative action is not likely before the spring 1973 session of the legislature.

Whatever the reaction is to be, the Worth Report is now the only major force for liberal reform in Alberta education. And a formidable force it is likely to be. Four men now share the leadership mantle: the members of the Cabinet Committee on Education (Lou Hyndman and Jim Foster, both young aggressive lawyers, and Bert Hohol, a professional educational administrator) together with Walter H. Worth whose report may well stand education in Alberta on its ear.

Euphoria in British Columbia Education—Let's Wait and See

John F. Ellis

"What a difference a day makes!" wrote Adam Robertson, President of the B.C. Teachers' Federation. He was recalling his sense of elation when the results of the provincial election of August 30, 1972, became apparent. The seemingly unbeatable W. A. C. Bennett and his Social Credit Party had been swept from office by what Bennett called "The Socialist Hordes"—the N.D.P. led by social worker David Barrett.

The Bennett government had been determined to slow the rate of educational expenditures and had achieved notable success. Citing data prepared by the Economic Council of Canada which suggested that the costs of health, welfare, and education would consume the entire G.N.P. by the end of the century. Bennett had held 1972 per pupil costs to 6.1 per cent over 1971. This was in contrast with the 14.8 per cent annual compound rate for the period 1958 to 1968.

In the meantime, the B.C. Teachers' Federation had become increasingly vocal in its criticisms of fiscal policies affecting education. In April of 1972 the teachers moved beyond words and established a political action fund of $1.2 million (one day's pay per member) with the stated purpose of defeating the Socreds at the August election. Arms were twisted and the money rolled in.

With a box score on August 30 of N.D.P.–36, Liberals–5, Conservatives–2, Socred–10, the B.C.T.F. Executive, particularly its militant wing, was understandably euphoric.

To achieve a slowdown in cost increases, the former Minister of Education, Donald Brothers, had developed a fourfold and extremely powerful control mechanism. First, government grants were paid to school districts on the basis of instructional units (groups of 20 secondary or 30 elementary pupils) rather than being based on the qualification and experience levels of the teachers in the district. Second, although school boards might under certain conditions obtain approval to exceed the approved basic program budget by up to 8 per cent and still obtain sharing grants from Victoria, proposed expenditures beyond this amount had to be approved by local taxpayers and paid for entirely from local revenue. Third, capital expenditures required local voter approval. However, the Department of Education could retard this process because it had to approve the introduction of the local by-law and then, it authorized the actual borrowing of funds if the by-law passed. Finally, the Provincial Government was empowered to establish annually a "fair and reasonable increase in teachers' salaries which the government will accept as shareable expense." A school board exceeding the set figure had to obtain all of the excess locally after receiving ratepayer approval. Mr. Brothers had said that 6.5 per cent was a "fair and reasonable increase" for 1972.

It was this later action that lit the fuse. Teachers believed that they had been singled out for unfair and repressive treatment in being made the first target of an embryonic wage control policy. Although their political war chest had been frozen by a court injunction, sought and obtained by two of their colleagues, many individual teachers used their summer holidays to lick stamps, answer telephones, and ring doorbells–most, apparently, on behalf of the N.D.P.

Naturally, the leaders of the B.C.T.F. like to think that they were a major factor in getting rid of Mr. Bennett. Nevertheless, whatever the reason for the N.D.P. victory (or the Socred loss), education issues were not prominent in the election campaign. In fact, none of the four parties was able to articulate an education platform that gained any substantial measure of public attention.

The reason for this might have been that earlier in 1972, B.C. newspaper readers were the bemused onlookers during the "Battle of the Graphs." For several weeks, first the Teachers' Federation and then the Minister of Education took full page ads to "prove" by means of line graphs, bar graphs, circle graphs, either the miserliness or the munificence of the Provincial Government in its treatment of the schools. This rather sad little exercise was brought to a hilarious conclusion by Len Norris, the outstanding *Vancouver Sun* cartoonist, who published his own set of "graphs" on various "public issues." He successfully captured the public mood: citizens were getting tired of skirmishes between politicians and teachers because each group seemed more concerned with vindicating itself than with dealing with the major issue–the determination of the shape and direction of public education.

About one matter there was widespread agreement: the schools were costing too much. Or perhaps it would be more accurate to say that the public believed that it was paying too much for what it was getting.

It was at this point, of course, that the consensus disappeared and the full spectrum of educational ideologies emerged. On the one extreme there were those who urged the abandonment of a centralized system and the creation of community schools or of private "free" schools with local decision-making on all matters such as curriculum and organization–together with a broadening of the school's social responsibilities to include day-care centres, evening recreation, and health care. On the other extreme were those who favoured a return to "basic" education, who pointed with some justification at declining levels of student performance in reading, computation, and factual knowledge and who blamed the permissiveness of schools and teachers for all manner of social ills.

But the more typical reaction of the average citizen appeared to be at neither of these extremes. He was not convinced that higher expenditures automatically improved educational quality. He was not at all sure that innovation was automatically a good thing. He was increasingly suspicious of educational experts who propounded the virtues of their pet hobby horses–sensitivity training, open area schools, voluntary attendance, discovery learning, creative experiences. He had gone along with the experts in the past and it had always cost money and seldom seemed to have made much difference to his child or his neighbour's child. He was starting to question the unstated motives of the social engineers, the counsellors, and the professors who seemed to be trying to turn his child into a different kind of social being–without ever seeking permission to do so. And he no longer believed that more education automatically opened the door to the "good life"–a life of higher wages, better jobs, more happiness, and greater fulfilment.

In short, Mr. Average Citizen was a pretty confused person. He still wanted the best for his children and he was probably prepared to pay for it. But he didn't know what to buy and nobody seemed to be helping him to find out. Least of all the Teachers' Federation and the government.

This was the educational context prior to August 30, 1972.

Premier Barrett's announcement that Eileen Dailly was to be Minister of Education as well as Deputy Premier was well received. She had been the articulate expert on education for the N.D.P. in opposition. She had been a school trustee, a primary school teacher and an outspoken supporter of causes such as the need for smaller classes, the abolition of corporal punishment, and improved services for children with learning disabilities.

Moreover, unlike her predecessor she was a good listener and was accessible. As a result, the Department of Education has experienced a flood of visitors and correspondence quite unlike that ever seen before by senior officials. New ideas, old ideas, good ones, bad ones, new complaints, old complaints, self-seekers, well-wishers, tale-bearers, those with axes to grind, those with services to offer, all have descended upon Victoria. And Mrs. Dailly personally has met an amazingly high proportion of them.

Furthermore, individuals and groups who meet with the minister comment on her concern for educational matters and her frankness. Adam Robertson's reaction is typical,"Perhaps the most heartening thing about the meeting is that teachers, trustees and government could sit down together and discuss these problems in an open and frank atmosphere for the first time in many years."

There is no question that the educational climate has been greatly improved thanks to Mrs. Dailly. In addition, the brief session of the legislature held in October repealed certain legislation that was offensive to the teachers. The statutory limitation on salary increases was removed (the teachers subsequently negotiated increases averaging 9.1 per cent rather than Donald Brothers' 6.5 per cent). School districts were allowed to exceed basic program costs by 10 per cent rather than 8 per cent. And about $600,000 of supplementary grants was made available to certain school districts to improve essential services. (Essential services did not include painting buildings as one school board was reminded.)

Mrs. Dailly has also announced that kindergartens are to be province-wide. She has shrewdly and quite properly announced a $10 million capital appropriation for the regional colleges which the Socreds tucked into last year's budget and rather unwisely failed to mention. She has given Andy Soles, Superintendent of Post Secondary Services, more elbow room by separating his division from the other divisions in the Department of Education which are more concerned with the public school system.

All of this represents a very good record of achievement for a new government and a new minister. But even the most charitably disposed realize that all that has really been achieved thus far is the removal of some relatively minor irritants, the stating of some noble intentions, and the creation of a more harmonious climate.

The real work and the tough decisions lie ahead. An able politician like Eileen Dailly knows that it is not enough to state good intentions. Clear thinking, expert advice, careful planning, and money–all in large quantities–are required. The money will come from the $500 million Socred surplus, presumably. For the remainder, she is counting heavily on the reports of the two Commissions–Public School and Post Secondary–she has announced but has not yet named. In this regard, it may well be that time will be the greatest enemy of the minister. Commission reports take a long time to prepare. Participatory democracy is a painfully slow process as any university president will testify. Mrs. Dailly will soon find herself in a painful bind between the N.D.P. promise to consult widely and the politician's need to produce results.

Looking to the future, central versus local control in education may well prove to be one of the most delicate and explosive issues that the government will have to handle. Already there are indications that the universities and colleges, which up to now have enjoyed great autonomy, will be subject to a central co-ordinating agency of some sort. In fact, it may not be long before some academics will recall the Bennett-Socred days with some nostalgia. Fiscal arrangements might have been somewhat arbitrary but at least no one asked very searching questions about budgets, new programs, facility utilization and request for capital money.

In the public school system the local control/central control problem will be somewhat more complex. Consider the following sets of dilemmas. The N.D.P. favours the abolition of local taxation for school purposes; it believes that local teachers' groups should negotiate salaries with locally elected trustees; and it has removed statutory limitations on salary increases. Will the government be prepared to let a local board freely contract to spend money it did not raise? Mrs. Dailly has expressed admiration for schools that develop their own curriculum, education, counselling, library service, and special education and she is in favour of the local appointment of school superintendents. How will the government determine if its intentions are being carried out in a given district? Will it be necessary to create a second layer of provincial school inspectors to watchdog the local ones? It will be fascinating to watch how deftly Eileen Dailly handles the dilemmas and conflicts implicit in the foregoing. Or perhaps she will come to believe that he who pays the educational piper calls the tune.

In all of this, there is a dawning awareness among teachers and trustees that some difficult days lie ahead. The teachers no longer have their whipping boy, Mr. Bennett. Accordingly, they must shift from confrontation to construction–a difficult transition, as recent years have shown. The trustees have lost much of the statutory protection against escalating costs that Mr. Brothers had developed and some are concerned that the balance of power may have shifted in favour of the teachers.

As we said at the beginning, education in British Columbia is a bit euphoric these days. But so far all we have had is a short dress rehearsal and good advance ticket sales. The actors are in place, the houselights are dimmed and the curtain is about to go up on Act I. Let's sit back and watch.

About The Contributors

Michael Katz teaches history of education at the Ontario Institute for Studies in Education.

Ioan Davies teaches sociology at York University.

Hugh Stevenson teaches history at Althouse College at the University of Western Ontario.

Howard Fluxgold is a research assistant for the Ontario Teachers' Federation.

Douglas Myers is on loan to the Ontario Teachers' Federation from the Ontario Institute for Studies in Education, where he teaches history of education.

Eric Hillis is doing graduate studies in the Faculty of Education, University of Alberta, on leave from the Atlantic Institute of Education in Halifax.

David Beard, a former teacher, runs Cine Books, a Toronto Bookshop devoted entirely to the subject of film.

Albert Tucker is Principal of Glendon College, York University.

Fiona Nelson, a former teacher, is Vice-Chairman of the Toronto Board of Education.

Don MacIver is Dean of Education of the University of New Brunswick.

Ron Faris heads the General Studies Division, Extension Department, University of Saskatchewan, Regina.

Walter Pitman, former MPP and education critic for the New Democratic Party of Ontario, is Dean of Arts and Science at Trent University.

Norman Henchey teaches in the Faculty of Education of McGill University.

Peter McCreath teaches history at Sir John A. Macdonald High School, Fire Island Lake, Nova Scotia.

Gordon McIntosh is Assistant Dean of the Faculty of Education, University of Alberta.

Jim Small and Robert Bryce teach in the Department of Education Administration, Faculty of Education, University of Alberta.

John Ellis teaches in the Faculty of Education at Simon Fraser University, British Columbia.